GREAT
CAT STORIES

Memorable Tales of Remarkable Cats

ROXANNE WILLEMS SNOPEK

VICTORIA · VANCOUVER · CALGARY

Heritage House Publishing Company Ltd.
www.heritagehouse.ca

Library and Archives Canada Cataloguing in Publication
Snopek, Roxanne Willems
   Great cat stories: Memorable Tales of Remarkable Cats
Roxanne Willems Snopek. — 1st Heritage House ed.

(Amazing stories)
Issued also in electronic formats.
ISBN 978-1-926613-96-3

   1. Cats—Canada—Anecdotes. 2. Cat owners—Canada—Anecdotes.
I. Title. II. Series: Amazing stories (Surrey, B.C.)

SF445.5.S66 2011   636.8'0887   C2010-906912-9

Series editor: Lesley Reynolds.
Cover design: Chyla Cardinal. Interior design: Frances Hunter.
Cover photo: Dmitry Naumov/iStockphoto.
Excerpts from *Mister Got-to-Go* with permission of Red Deer Press. Chapter Nine, The Simon Years, originally appeared in *Reader's Digest* and appears in this book in altered form. Copyright © 2002 by Reader's Digest Magazines Limited. Reprinted by permission from the March 2002 issue of *Reader's Digest* and the author, Roxanne Willems Snopek.

The interior of this book was printed on 100% post-consumer recycled paper, processed chlorine free and printed with vegetable-based inks.

Heritage House acknowledges the financial support for its publishing program from the Government of Canada through the Canada Book Fund (CBF), Canada Council for the Arts and the province of British Columbia through the British Columbia Arts Council and the Book Publishing Tax Credit.

  Canada Council   Conseil des Arts
for the Arts   du Canada   BRITISH COLUMBIA
ARTS COUNCIL   Canadian   Patrimoine
Heritage   canadien

14 13 12 11   1 2 3 4 5
Printed in Canada

GREAT
CAT STORIES

In memory of our old boy Cody.
We miss you, Cody-cat.

Contents

Prologue

TREES TURN COLOUR EARLY IN *Saskatchewan, and fall is just a quick slip of a season before winter's cold arrives to stay. The veterinary teaching hospital where I worked was across the bridge from my apartment. Although the drive to work was short and pretty, my job was anything but. Until an animal health technician position opened up, where I could use my newly acquired skills, I was stuck on kennel duty and I hated it.*

I quickly cleaned and fed the patients in the cat ward. Then I moved to the large dog runs. Hot water shot out of the hose, sending excrement and bits of food rolling down the trough to the drain at the end. Even with my nose clamped shut, I could taste the smell at the back of my throat, and I knew it clung to my clothing when I went home.

Finally I came to the smaller cages on the dog ward. It was quiet that day, and I progressed quickly until I came to the last cage. Inside, to my astonishment, crouched a tiny kitten, thin and filthy, its eyes crusted and running. Too young to be away from its mother, but not old enough to be vaccinated, this kitten was in the no-man's land of infectious disease. And he'd been abandoned.

I cleaned him up as best I could, but he was just a baby and a messy one at that. His coat was stained and matted from one end to the other, and when I set down his dish of warm gruel I saw why. He promptly climbed right in, slurping and kneading the dish with his paws as if he knew he should still be nursing at his mother's side.

I hoped he'd find a home, but I knew his chances were slim. There was no way I could take him; my apartment was strictly "No Pets." If he were at least cute, there was a chance someone would take pity on him. But he was sickly, dirty, noisy and ugly. Who would want such a kitten?

1

Lost . . . and Found

"Cats seem to go on the principle that it never does any harm to ask for what you want." —JOSEPH WOOD KRUTCH

MID-LIFE IS A TIME OF CHANGE. Some people find themselves letting go of parts of their lives that no longer fit. Some discover a sudden yearning to fulfill long-forgotten dreams. And for some people it's a matter of adapting to the unexpected, both good and bad.

Barb Taylor of Cumberland, Ontario, didn't choose change in her life; change chose her. It began with a dream—to build a new home. This decision was not entered into lightly; Barb can count on one hand the number of times she's moved in 56 years. "At 19, I hopped a plane and headed west from England," she says. "I told my parents I was going to stay in Canada for two years whether I liked it or not. That was 1968. I've never looked back."

Barb's life was good, but busy. Her husband's work kept him away from home much of the time. Until recently, Barb's job as an administrative assistant in a high-tech company had kept her preoccupied with the lives of others. "The hours were long, and the pay was short," she says wryly. When she left her job, she was finally able to put her energy toward managing the life she shared with her husband and Benji, her Bichon Frise dog. She was settled and content, looking forward to the next phase of her life and marriage.

"My life was my garden, my ordinary, everyday stuff, and my Benji," she says with a laugh. "I am so boring." But change was stalking her. Around that time, Barb's husband's business partner passed away, leaving a beautiful piece of property overlooking the Ottawa River. His widow wanted to sell it to them. Barb's first reaction was resistance. "It was too expensive and much farther away than we wanted to move," recalls Barb. "But it was gorgeous. And it got the building bug going in us." Once the idea bit, it hung on. Her husband broke down her initial defences, and soon Barb caught his excitement. They found a different lot, in an area they liked and in the price range they'd hoped for, and started making plans to build their dream home.

It was an exciting and exhausting time. Moving out of the house they'd lived in for more than 20 years was more difficult in every way than Barb had imagined it would be. A lot of living had gone on within its walls; they'd been the backdrop for memories both good and bad—the whole range of experiences that make up a life together. She knew it would be some time before the new house, beautiful as it was, would feel like home to them. Finally the last nail was in place, and in February of 1999 they moved in. She looked forward to quiet evenings, enjoying some peace and contentment reconnecting with each other.

But before Barb had even finished unpacking all the boxes, she was blindsided by a stunning twist: her husband of 28 years left her. The shock was devastating. Everything she believed was called into question, and she found herself withdrawing, trying to hide from the pain. "It was hard," she remembers. "This wasn't supposed to be *my* dream house; it was supposed to be *our* dream house." Instead, she found herself in a new house, a new neighbourhood and alone.

Except for Benji, her lifeline. "He was a cuddler," says Barb, "a very human sort of dog." Recurrent knee problems had made Benji dependent on Barb to carry him around, and he enjoyed being pampered. He also had diabetes, which meant Barb was responsible for giving him twice-daily insulin injections and monitoring his food intake. Having Benji to care for during that time helped her get through the worst of it. She was able to push aside her own vulnerability and focus on his needs. But Benji was 13 years old. Barb knew his days with her were limited.

In September of that year, the time she'd been dreading arrived: Benji died. Now Barb was truly alone, and she began to feel the full impact of the loss that walked hand-in-hand with the changes in her life. Barb forced herself to be strong and think positively. At least, she told herself, she'd had time to prepare for Benji's death. He'd had a good life. She'd cared well for him at the end, and she'd said her goodbyes. Now it was time to move on. She desperately tried not to dwell on her sense of loss. She looked around her beautiful new home at the cherry hardwood floors, gleaming countertops and black furniture and told herself that, in spite of missing Benji, she'd be happy not to have white dog hair all over the house anymore.

No matter how hard she tried to ignore it, however, she knew something was missing from her life. "Having never had children, I was finding my life, to say the least, pretty empty," recalls Barb. "However, I worked at putting away all the doggy things, returned the unused insulin, and said to myself, 'Okay Barbie, put the vacuum away. You can come and go as you please. You only have yourself to take care of now.'"

Her bittersweet freedom lasted until the following spring. It was a beautiful Friday evening in May, and Barb was just about to have her supper, a symbolic meal celebrating her independence. "I'm pretty self-sufficient now," she says with a grin, "but before I'd always let the men handle the barbecue. That evening, I'd made up my mind to cook myself a steak." Much to her satisfaction, she turned out a perfectly grilled chunk of sizzling sirloin.

Her habit, since becoming single again, was to eat standing

in front of the kitchen window, looking into her backyard. But before the first tasty bite reached her lips, she saw a strange animal meandering aimlessly across her yard.

This, in itself, was no surprise. To her great delight, Barb had discovered her new semi-rural neighbourhood to be populated with many wild animals, including raccoons, foxes, groundhogs, fishers and birds of all sorts. Her kitchen window provided an endlessly entertaining glimpse into the natural world. This furtive stranger, however, was not a wild animal. It was a cat, a grey and white tabby, and his erratic progress triggered her concern. "He didn't look like he knew where he was going," she recalls. "He seemed lost and con-fused, as if he'd been wandering around for awhile." As he picked his way around the pool toward the open garage door, Barb suddenly remembered the mousetraps she'd set earlier. She left her dinner untasted and ran outside to head him off.

Her reaction wasn't due to an abiding affection for cats. Barb had always felt that, when compared to Benji, cats didn't even rate. After all, they shed everywhere, they scratched the furniture, they were selfish and independent, not to mention the little issue of hairballs. "I was definitely not a cat person," Barb emphasizes. "I knew the nose and the tail, that's it." She simply reacted on instinct, hoping to shoo him away before he hurt himself. But as soon as she came near, before she'd even touched him, the cat abandoned his wily ways, dropped down and rolled onto his side, beg-ging her to pet him. She didn't quite know what to think.

"Aren't cats afraid of strangers?" she asked herself. "From that moment," she says, "I realized this cat was different."

She saw that he was a young male, not neutered, and hungry but not starved. He obviously had a home somewhere. But wherever he came from, it had been too long since his last meal. So she invited him in. "What do cats eat?" she wondered. Having no intention of sharing her very first steak, she crossed her fingers and opened a can of tuna for him. "I was worried about making him sick," she says. "Benji had had a very sensitive stomach, so I was used to being careful. But this cat ate the whole can without hesitation and looked at me as if to say 'thank you.'" He seemed rather nice, she thought—for a cat.

She began phoning around to see if any neighbourhood cats had gone missing. "The Ottawa Senators were playing their final hockey game that night," she remembers, "so I knew a lot of my neighbours would be home watching it on television." One cat-loving friend asked her to bring the stray over so she could take a look at him. Barb scooped up the little cat and carried him over. He lay calmly in her arms, but when the friend reached for him, he leaped down and refused to come back. She cajoled and sweet-talked, but he wouldn't come near them. "Everyone told me not to worry," says Barb. "It's a cat, they told me. It'll go home." So she went back home and went to bed, firmly ignoring her concern. The next morning it was raining, and she wondered if he'd been able to find someplace dry. She called for him outside but didn't see him. He must have found his way home, she told herself. But she kept thinking about him, hoping he was okay. On Sunday morning she went out again and looked for him. This time she spotted him in the tall grass at the side of her yard; when she called to him, he came.

Barb immediately put him in a crate and took him to the veterinarian to make sure he was healthy. They looked for tattoos or microchips that might be used to reunite him with his owner, but he had no identification. Worse still, they discovered an infected toe. During his travels, the little cat had somehow torn his claw so badly it was now on the verge of gangrene. He needed antibiotics. And until that treatment was finished he couldn't be vaccinated.

None of this was good news. Barb filled the prescription, paid the bill and reluctantly returned home with the cat in his crate beside her. Neither of them was happy. Suddenly the car was filled with a horrible odour. "He'd peed inside his little crate, all over himself. I'd covered the carrier with a towel, thank goodness, or I'd have been showered too."

The urine of an intact male cat is a powerful identification tool, used to mark territory and warn away competition. But to the human nose, especially in close quarters, the smell is sinus-searingly nasty, potent enough to take your breath away. Barb couldn't bring such a stench into the house, but she couldn't leave the cat outside with his injured toe, either. "I knew he'd clean himself off eventually, but what were we supposed to do in the meantime?" Cats aren't known to love water, but it didn't matter. They eyed each other warily, but Barb knew there was only one solution. "I had to wash him," she confesses.

She rolled up her sleeves, plugged her nose and hauled him to the laundry room sink. The cat didn't like it, but Barb gave him no choice. "I was bound and determined," she says. "The poor guy didn't have a chance. In the end, I won. But I had to wipe down the walls and floor afterwards." He was shampooed, scrubbed, rinsed and rubbed until at last the odour was gone and he could be allowed into the house again. As soon as she finished, he sprang away to dry off and recover his injured dignity. They were both exhausted.

Once she had time to sit down and consider her options, Barb found herself in a dilemma. She'd found a cat rescue agency named Friends of Abandoned Pets (FOAP), but they had no foster homes available just then. Even if one had been available, this unvaccinated stray presented a potential health risk to the other cats and would be best kept by himself until his health status was certain.

Friends of Abandoned Pets first suggested that Barb sign on to be the foster home; they would then assume responsibility for his veterinary bills and look for a permanent home. "This meant," explains Barb, "that I'd probably have him for quite a long time before he was adoptable." She feared that after caring for him, she might become attached to him only to have to give him up eventually because—as a foster care provider—Barb would be ineligible to adopt him herself. Barb wavered; she wasn't about to risk opening her heart again, only to be hurt and alone in the end. Then the FOAP counsellor suggested Barb could keep her options open by taking full responsibility (including financial) for him while she searched for his owners. "And, of course," she says, "that's what I did."

Barb continued to hope that somewhere out there a family was searching for their beloved missing pet. She was convinced he must have been something special to someone. "I spent the next couple of weeks trying to find an owner." She called several local shelters and rescue organizations, but no one had reported a missing cat of his description. She was afraid to relinquish him to a municipal shelter because, despite their assurances that all adoptable pets find homes, she knew there was a risk he'd end up being put to sleep. "He was such a nice cat. I was positive he belonged to somebody," she says.

Barb wondered why she felt such an obligation to help this unfortunate stray who'd found his way into her yard. She certainly hadn't been looking for a cat. But, for the time being at least, she was stuck with him. "I tried hard to find him a good home," says Barb. "I didn't believe mine was the right place for him." She tried not to feel any further responsibility. After all, she'd fed him. She'd paid to have him patched up. She'd even bathed him. Why should she feel obligated to give him a home too? Surely some cat lover out there would recognize what a nice boy he was and take him home. She tried to give him to her neighbours. She tried to give him to family members. There had to be a way to find a good home for this lovely cat. But that would *not*, she insisted to herself, be *her* home. She wanted her freedom; she didn't want to be vacuuming up cat hair.

But the whole time she was trying so hard to foist him on someone else, she knew that deeper things were at work in her heart. She'd never forget the heartbreak she'd felt when Benji died. She was still reeling from the breakup of her marriage. She'd had enough loss recently; she wasn't ready for any more. But perhaps taking risks was part of the healing process. She knew that if she looked after this little stray much longer she'd be too attached to give him up. Her heart would once more be at risk.

So she continued her efforts to find his original home. Somewhere along the way, for no particular reason, she began to call him Sammy. Now, cat lovers everywhere know that once you name something, it's yours. The jig was up, but Barb wasn't ready to admit this to herself yet.

"I posted pictures all over the neighbourhood mailboxes," she says, "even though we aren't supposed to do that." The woman at the post office told her the area was known to be a dumping ground for unwanted animals. Thoughtless owners found the semi-rural roads a convenient place to casually "lose" inconvenient pets. "Go ahead and put up your pictures," said the post-office lady. "I'm not supposed to allow it, but I'll close my eyes."

"I believe Sammy was sent to me." BARB TAYLOR

Still no one responded. But soon afterwards, she noticed that someone else had posted a picture of another cat, a female, found on the same night as Sammy. Immediately, she phoned the number. The story she heard was so similar to the way she found Sammy that she began to think the post-office lady might have had it right. Had someone taken two unwanted cats to the country and left them there to fend for themselves as best they could? "Who knows?" says Barb. Too many cats find themselves set free to starve or be killed by predators when their owners decide to join the spring moving frenzy. The little female cat ended up at the humane society, hopefully to be adopted, but Barb refused to take that chance with Sammy.

She continued her efforts at locating his owners, or at least finding someone who wanted to give him a good home, until finally someone told her bluntly that Sammy didn't need a good home because he already had one: with her. Barb had to face what was already evident to everyone else around her. Not only had she become a cat owner, but—without noticing it, without even wanting it—she'd become a cat lover too. Soon after, while visiting a friend who had two dogs and two cats, she realized just how much she'd changed because of Sammy. "Normally in the past I would have gone to pat the dogs first and ignored the cats," she says with a laugh. "Now I say hello to the cats first, and *then* go pat the dogs."

"I'd never have believed I'd ever have a cat in my home. I don't even wear angora because the fluffy stuff bugs me so much. Did I realize how much a cat sheds? Oh, my! I have dark hardwood floors and there's cat hair everywhere." But Sammy, it seems, knew he had won Barb over. His goal accomplished, he has settled down and is enjoying the quiet life that suits them both so well. As for Barb, she finds it hard to believe how much she's enjoying this unexpected turn of events. "I think this little guy had a lucky day when he 'found' me," says Barb. "But, even more important, I'm a very lucky person."

Barb has proven herself to Sammy as well, giving a lot of security to her new companion. "He fell down the stairs once," she remembers. "It's an open-tread staircase and he was trying to jump to a window. He missed and fell about 20 feet onto the ceramic-tile floor below." To her relief, he wasn't injured, but that incident made her shudder to think of him taking a similar fall into one of the rocky crevasses near her home. The risks, she decided, were too great. Now Sammy enjoys the outdoors by birdwatching at the windows. Pine siskins and American goldfinches give him hours of entertainment, and neither he nor his little friends are in danger.

She's also getting to know Sammy's temperament. "He's easily spooked," she says. "If he hears a strange voice in the house, even a soft-spoken female voice, he disappears." But Sammy seems to understand that Barb has accepted him wholeheartedly. It's finally safe for him to relax and just be himself with her.

Barb's heart is vulnerable once more, but the love Sammy brings is worth it. She knows there's no avoiding the twists and turns of life. But sometimes the most unwelcome changes lead to surprising joy. "Someone must have thought I needed somebody to take care of," says Barb. "In hindsight, I believe Sammy was sent to me." It seems that Barb's new house has finally become home, thanks to the little cat that insisted he belonged there too.

CHAPTER

2

The Cold, Hostile Streets

"Time spent with cats is never wasted." —COLETTE

FOR LINDA JEAN GUBBE OF Saskatoon, Saskatchewan, it all started in 1996. "I was working downtown at the time," she says, "and when I left the office for my lunch break I noticed some cats hanging around outside." Two in particular caught her eye, one grey and one black and white. She began going outside on her breaks to look for them and soon discovered they lived beneath the building. She didn't always see them, but they saw her, especially after she began putting down dishes of food. "They started to know what time I'd come, and I'd see eyes watching me."

As they became accustomed to her presence, Linda was able to observe them a bit more closely; she began to take note of how many there were, which ones were pregnant, and if any of them appeared ill. They didn't let her get close to them, so there wasn't much she could do but watch and bring food.

But for Linda, a fire had been lit. "You know how it is— all of a sudden one day you become aware of something, for whatever reason, and then you start seeing it everywhere?" So many cats lived in the cracks and crannies of the city. And not just her city. She began to search out organizations that worked with feral cats and discovered that many other people had the same concerns she did—and were doing something about it. If others were doing it, thought Linda, she could too. "I'm not a very patient person," admits Linda with a laugh. "I like to get things done." A few short months later, Street Cat Rescue of Saskatoon, also known by its nickname SCAT, was up and running. "We were registered at the beginning of 1997," she comments with pride.

Inspired by hope. Guided by compassion. That's the phrase above the logo on the SCAT website. Linda and her volunteers at SCAT have a two-part mission: to reduce the at-large feral cat population through non-lethal control and to promote public awareness of responsible companion-animal guardianship and compassion for feral cats in the community.

They're lofty goals, but Linda has a lot of support, especially from her family. Long-time animal lovers themselves, her parents knew the importance of what Linda was trying to do and that she'd do it with or without their help. "Mom was the most help at the beginning; Dad just said, 'More cats?'" But no charitable organization can survive without behind-the-scenes practical assistance, and that's where Linda's dad shone. If anything needed to be built—a shelter or a cat run—he was there with hammer and nails. "He even became a member," says Linda, "because he was proud of his daughter." But the real surprise was when, after helping Linda feed that first colony of ferals she'd noticed beneath her work building, his heart was stolen. "He'd never had a cat of 'his own,' but this little tortoiseshell just fell in love with him. He called her Cuddles, and she went home with him eventually."

The cat that personifies what SCAT is all about is a little ginger shorthair the volunteers dubbed Fantasia because of the amazing trip they found she had survived in order to get to Saskatoon. "Sometime in July of 1997, early in SCAT's history, I received a call from a woman who said this little cat had been found up inside the motor of her husband's semi," recalls Linda. He had to take his engine apart to get at her, and when he was finally able to pull her out she was no prize: filthy, oily, scruffy, with raw, sore-looking ears. And she was very fat. But as soon as she knew she was safe, her delighted purrs made it obvious that she had once been a well-loved pet. The trucker called SCAT and put the ginger cat in his garage to await Linda's arrival. "We went over and found this very dirty, very sweet, very pregnant little orange tabby with these mysterious sores on her ears." It looked to

Linda like recent frostbite. But that was hardly possible—it was the middle of a blistering prairie summer.

"About an hour later," continues Linda, "the woman called back." She reported that her husband had gone back to work and was discussing the little cat when one of the other truckers spoke up. "That must be the one that jumped out of the back of my truck." She had scurried out of the trailer, and he had not been able to catch her. The last he'd seen of her, she was in among the other trucks. He'd just completed a long trip from Calgary, Alberta . . . hauling a refrigerator trailer.

The mysteries of her frostbitten ears and her long journey were solved, but there still remained the question of where this tough little cat belonged. SCAT members began contacting Calgary shelters and rescue groups in the hope of finding her family. They wanted to get her home before she gave birth. Unfortunately, no one had reported her missing, so Fantasia's kittens were born at the shelter. The volunteers felt sorry for her, being separated from her home, but at least these babies would grow up with love and care, instead of on the street, wild and unwanted.

"A week or so later a call came in about four kittens, a week old, whose feral mom had been scared away and hadn't returned," relates Linda. They'd found a volunteer willing to try bottle-feeding, but round-the-clock kitten-raising is hard work, and she felt she could only handle two of them. The other two orphans were brought to the shelter on the off chance that Fantasia would be willing to add them to her little family.

"We knew there was a chance she might reject them," says Linda. "So we took the two new kittens and rubbed them alongside Fantasia's kittens before putting them in the basket." Then they held their breath as they set the foundlings next to the other kittens. "We needn't have bothered," says Linda. "We had just barely dropped them into the basket before she was trying to clean them. She immediately gave the two new kittens a complete bath and tucked them in with the others. She was an amazing mom as well as a travelling girl." Fantasia's amazing journey ended in a new life for her and four kittens saved from a life on the street. "They have all since been adopted into great homes, but they are ever in our minds as one of our best success stories."

Today, Linda's work is more at the podium than it is in the trenches. Her vast network of 200 volunteers is more than capable of handling the work in the streets and alleys. "My area is primarily paperwork—talking to media, talking to people, going into schools, so I can find other volunteers, raise awareness and find money and resources to pass on to the people who need it."

Many feral cats weren't always wild; they may have had human families and homes at one time. Then, for one reason or another, they found themselves out on the street. Cats, being the resourceful species they are, often cling to survival by learning to scrounge and hunt, but this behaviour seldom endears them to people. Thieving from garbage pails, stalking bird feeders and nipping into the food bag in the garage earns them little more than a bad reputation. Their soft fur and gentle demeanour quickly disappear, replaced by dirt, scars and a watchful, lean and hungry look. Such cats seldom receive a warm neighbourhood welcome. It doesn't take long for trust to erode, but still, these are usually stray cats, not true ferals. When these former pets not only survive, but also reproduce, the instinct to protect their offspring leads them to give birth in such tucked-away places that their babies have virtually no human contact. When they emerge with their mothers several weeks after birth, they look on the world through eyes untouched by domestication. These kittens belong to the race of domestic felines, but they are essentially wild. Unless caught and rehabilitated early, they will become true feral cats, living short, hard lives and producing more kittens before dying on the cold streets.

Linda wants to break this cycle. "It's hard to reduce feral populations," she says. A vital part of breaking the cycle is preventing the birth of more feral kittens. SCAT promotes the use of TNR (Trap, Neuter, Return) whenever it's in the best interest of the particular cat, but their preferred plan is something they call TNFA or Trap, Neuter, Foster, Adopt. Live traps are used to catch the cats without harming them. Then they are spayed or neutered and evaluated for temperament. If the cats are truly wild, they are returned to their colony. If there are any indications that the cat is willing to rejoin civilization, it's placed in a foster home to await permanent adoption.

"What I envision for SCAT isn't just taking care of colonies," says Linda. "I wanted a key part of our work to be providing a resource base for other caregivers." Many individuals are working quietly to care for the feral cats in their neighbourhood, but they don't necessarily know the importance of doing it properly. People who don't like cats don't differentiate between feral cats, strays and the cat next door. Leaving food out, for instance, can attract unwanted wildlife and irritate neighbours. "People get annoyed by the cat that wanders into their yard and pees on their property. Ferals avoid people," she emphasizes. "They don't come into yards."

But Linda knows that improving the future for feral cats doesn't start with the cats. It starts with humans, and some humans have enough problems of their own without worrying about the needs of a cat.

The instant she answered the phone one day at the shelter, Linda had a feeling it would be bad news. The woman on the other end of the phone said she'd found a kitten starving in a dumpster. She had brought it inside, but now it wouldn't eat. Could Linda do something to help? Linda sighed silently and then began explaining that this kitten probably needed urgent veterinary care. Medical care is part of responsible pet ownership, she told the caller gently. But the woman refused to take the kitten to a veterinarian.

Her attitude was, "It's just a cat, and not even *my* cat. Can't *you* do something?"

Linda's biggest enemies are always ignorance, irresponsibility and apathy; this time was no different. As soon as she hung up the phone, she went to do what she could. "When an animal is sick or injured—especially a kitten—there's never any second thought," says Linda. "Just as soon as we have an address, we're out the door."

The address she was given confirmed her initial impression; it was a very neglected, rundown area of the city. The apartment building was even more derelict than she had expected. Linda and her partner walked up the rickety stairs, found the right number and knocked on the door. It was partly open, and they could hear the sound of a television inside, but no one came to the door. They heard whispering. Heads peered out from other doors then quickly ducked back inside. Still, no one answered. They were about to leave when someone in another apartment asked if they were there about the kitten. Once the neighbour realized they wanted to help, the atmosphere changed quite suddenly. "I think they thought we were with the police," says Linda. The relieved neighbour pointed to the right door and told them to go on in.

Inside the dingy room they found the kitten lying on a chair, too weak to even lift its head. The woman who'd called barely looked at them before turning her gaze back to the television. When Linda realized there was a toddler in the room with the woman, she guessed what had really

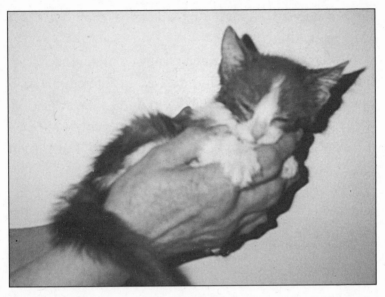

The Unsinkable Molly Brown as a kitten. LINDA JEAN GUBBE

happened. Small children often hurt kittens inadvertently by picking them up too roughly, perhaps by a limb or tail. Kittens and kids both need close supervision, especially when playing together.

They bundled up the little female kitten and took it straight to the animal hospital. She was terribly dehydrated, malnourished and too weak to even eat on her own. "But she had a will to live," says Linda. "When I held a spoon of food near her, her little mouth would open and close even though she couldn't lift her head, so I'd poke in some food." The kitten, who appeared to be eight or nine weeks old, needed to be hand-fed every hour for an entire week before she began to regain her strength. But she didn't give up. They began to call her The Unsinkable Molly Brown.

"She ended up at my mom's place," Linda says. Round-the-clock care brought her back from the brink of death, but it still took a full two weeks before she began to act like a normal kitten. "Then," laughs Linda, "she became a pain in the butt. Boy, did she have spunk!"

One day soon after that, the woman from the apartment phoned SCAT again to find out when she could get her kitten back. Linda was torn; she knew these people wanted the kitten, but it was her responsibility to ensure they would provide adequate care. Pets cost money, and she wanted them to understand that if they couldn't afford to meet the kitten's needs, perhaps they shouldn't keep her. Many people of limited means find ways to provide for their animals, even if it means personal sacrifice, because they value them as family members. Maybe this woman truly did care about the kitten. There was only one way to tell. "There was a $200 veterinary bill that had to be paid if they wanted her back," she reports. "I explained this to the woman, and we never heard from her again."

Shortly afterwards, a couple came into the shelter with an unusual request. They were looking for a kitten, and they weren't particular about colour or coat or sex or any other characteristic. The only thing they wanted was a kitten to match the name they'd already chosen. As soon as she heard the name, Linda knew The Unsinkable Molly Brown had found a home.

They wanted a cat named Kaos: "chaos" spelled with a K. "Boy," Linda told them, "do I have a cat for you!"

When cats and people come together like this, Linda knows all her work has been worthwhile. "Often adoptions just seem to match, as if they were destined to be. That's so satisfying. When people phone later and tell us how well it's going," she adds quietly, "that's very nice."

But the teamwork of her fellow cat lovers is just as satisfying to Linda. "I definitely couldn't do this by myself," she emphasizes. "There are so many others who willingly joined me with their commitment and dedication to these animals."

She even has a code phrase to call people to action. It came about after a volunteer called Linda late one night to say she thought she smelled smoke in the shelter. Linda immediately told her to start putting the cats into carriers; then she started calling volunteers. "Every time I got someone on the phone and said the words, 'Smoke at the shelter,' there were no questions, no hesitations," recalls Linda. "Twelve volunteers were at the shelter within ten minutes." As it turned out, the smell was due to a burntout fluorescent-light ballast in the gas station next door, but in talking with the firefighters, Linda discovered that they hadn't known there was an animal shelter in the area. "They immediately put us on their list, so if there are ever any problems in the future with a nearby business, they'll be sure to monitor the safety of our animals," says Linda.

Linda and her co-workers spend their time and energy

Molly Brown grown up—now named Kaos. CARMEN BREITKREUTZ

caring for felines who will never thank them. In fact, many of their charges would do everything possible to avoid them. But that doesn't matter to the dedicated volunteers at SCAT. They know the cats are not to blame. Every feral cat eking out an existence on the fringes of civilization is there because somewhere, sometime, a human being has discarded a pet like so much garbage. Linda can't change what's already been done, but she's determined to try and prevent it from happening again. And in the meantime, she gives as much care as she can to those cats already living on the cold, hostile streets.

3

The Secret of Simon Teakettle

*"There are many intelligent species in the universe.
They are all owned by cats."* —ANONYMOUS

BARBARA FLORIO GRAHAM DOESN'T LOOK like a woman
with a mysterious past. With over five decades of journal-
istic experience, one might expect the energetic Gatineau,
Quebec, writer to have long since lost the excitement of the
creative process. But no, not Bobbi. Her love affair with
writing and teaching is as strong as ever. Her career has
brought not just international recognition but gifts, cards
and boatloads of fan mail.

She does, however, have a secret: her biggest success is
due to an unexpected friendship with a cat named Simon.

When Bobbi moved from Chicago in 1967, she brought
along her beloved cat, Mysti. But shortly after their arrival,
Mysti died. "I felt terrible and decided I wouldn't get a cat

again because the feeling was too awful when she died."
However, she missed the easy companionship. Eventually
she decided to get another cat, but this time not bond so
closely with it. An older cat, she thought, would be much
safer emotionally. She would be strict, she decided, right
from the start. This cat would be just a cat to her, another
creature to share her home. Nothing more. "So I answered
an ad in the *Ottawa Citizen*," she recalls. The advertisement
said the cat in question was a domestic shorthair, black,
neutered and free. He seemed like a good fit except for one
thing: Bobbi had a perfect name picked out and this one was
already named Simon (his brother was Garfunkle).

She explains, "We had a little saying from Don Quixote
when I was growing up, about the pot calling the kettle
black. I'd always called a black cat a 'teakettle,' and said
if I ever had one I'd call him Teakettle." She shrugged her
shoulders and took him anyway. Simon was very fright-
ened at the change in his life. He slunk around the house,
hiding under furniture, scuttling behind doors. Bobbi
had to work to gain his trust. But little by little, Simon
responded. By the time he finally adjusted to Bobbi, her
battle for a reserved attitude was lost; he'd wormed his way
into her heart. "The ban on sleeping on my bed was lifted,"
she admits. Still, she hankered to use the name she'd imagined. First she tried calling him Simon the Teakettle, but
it didn't quite seem right. Then she happened upon Simon
Teakettle. "As soon as I said it, I knew it was the perfect

name." She had no idea the effect this name would have on her life and career.

Bobbi had been certain of her calling early in life. Her first story, submitted when she was nine years old, was printed in *Humpty Dumpty Magazine* and earned her the grand total of five dollars. At the age of 11, she sold a story to *Jack and Jill* for $10. "That's when I decided to be a writer," says Bobbi. "I'd like to know of anyone else who doubled their income in two years—before they hit puberty!"

She knew journalism was the right path for her in spite of the challenges of being a self-employed, freelance writer. At the time Simon Teakettle joined her life, Bobbi was writing a regular column for a small community newspaper on a volunteer basis, as a favour to the editor, on top of her other writing jobs. The paper was still short of material, but in spite of great reader response, Bobbi hesitated to contribute more. Then, on a whim, she wrote a cheeky little piece from the viewpoint of her cat, signed it Simon Teakettle and sent it in. To her surprise, the editor loved it. Bobbi made him swear to keep Simon Teakettle's identity a secret. "Originally it was so that people wouldn't realize I was writing half the paper," quips Bobbi. But it quickly turned into something more. People began to ask, "Who is this Simon Teakettle?" As the mystery gained momentum, someone on the local CBC radio station mentioned him. Soon Simon's words were quoted almost every week.

Despite Simon's growing celebrity, Bobbi didn't receive

a penny for the columns she and her cat wrote for the paper. So she started looking at possible paying markets for Simon's material. "In 1975, I took a poem 'he'd' written and sent it to *Cats Magazine,* and they took it," recalls Bobbi. "I began sending his stuff off to other radio stations, too."

Then the axe fell. The small community newspaper was purchased by a large weekly, and word came down that almost all the copy would be cut. The new owners weren't interested in any of the regular writers, except for one column: this spicy, funny column by the mysterious Simon Teakettle. "My own column was cut," Bobbi protests with mock outrage, "but they kept the Simon Teakettle column." Not only that, but Simon Teakettle would now be paid for his words, $15 each week. Simon had begun to earn his kitty litter.

In Simon Teakettle's voice, Bobbi began to write for other publications. She still wrote her own genuine articles and columns, but with the Simon Teakettle columns, something else emerged from her creativity. In her entertainment columns, for instance, she'd report properly on the highbrow events around town. But as Simon Teakettle, she'd mercilessly skewer anything pretentious. "I would be invited to these things to write seriously for my other columns, but he would take the same events and write from his humorous, sarcastic, superior-to-humans persona." And Simon got away with the most preposterous stunts, such as "sneaking under the skirts of the Governor General's wife at the opening of an exhibit."

Throughout the development of this alter ego, the bond between Bobbi and Simon continued to grow. He was more than just companionship for her; he was inspiration, a true muse. "Simon Teakettle was always the fun side of my writing," says Bobbi.

Simon Teakettle was becoming very well known, and Bobbi knew it was time to take the next step. "He was so big I worried that the name would be stolen, so I started my own company." She called it "Simon Teakettle, Ink." She explains, "'Ink' is a play on words: a symbol of the human-feline partnership. Ink means writing and ink means black." What does Simon think of this? "He owns it all. The company, the website, the email and the business account are all in the company name," reports Bobbi. "*He* is the bigwig—so of course he thinks *he's* incorporated."

In spite of his upward mobility, the real person behind the classy black cat remained a mystery. The only ones to know the truth were a few local CBC executives. "Simon's 'interviews' were always handled by me, on the phone," says Bobbi. "For the Halloween shows we did, I would begin by saying Simon wasn't available because he was still out trick-or-treating, but that he'd left a message for me to read. I handled other shows in a similar fashion."

Bobbi soon became known as "the lady who shares Simon Teakettle's typewriter." Later, as technology advanced, she became "the lady who shares Simon Teakettle's computer," and eventually "the lady who shares Simon Teakettle's office."

In 1981, Bobbi had Simon enter a contest on a new program from the CBC in Edmonton called *RSVP*. Host David Lennick and Simon exchanged letters, and soon Simon was a regular on the program. After four years of regular guest spots for Simon on *RSVP*, Bobbi was disappointed to learn that the show was being moved to Toronto. But soon after, Bobbi scheduled a workshop in Toronto, and she and Simon decided to look up the host. "Simon wrote to Lennick and said that if he'd provide a phone number, 'The Lady' would arrange a meeting," says Bobbi. "Lennick arrived at the meeting with a delightful stuffed mouse wearing a dress and bonnet as a gift for Simon. He told me he'd finally discovered my identity just before he left Edmonton, after an exhaustive search by his staff."

Friendships fostered by Simon appeared to be long lasting; even though Lennick hasn't worked for the CBC for many years, he and Bobbi remain friends. Many other well-known people at the CBC claim friendship with Simon Teakettle as well; cards and letters from Mary Lou Finlay, Vicki Gabereau and Jurgen Gothe are among his cherished mementoes.

Simon Teakettle's career was most definitely on the rise. He was a contestant on *The Radio Show*. He was included in Lennick's new program, *Night Camp*. He contributed to *Basic Black* and *Morningside* and was asked to exchange on-air letters with Bill Richardson's cat on the summer program *Cross Words*. Simon's letters appeared in the *Globe and Mail* and the *Toronto Star*. He was quoted in the Canadian book *Purring is My Business*. As well, he found his way into *The Bedside Book of Celebrity Gossip*, published in the United States by Crown Group. "Simon Teakettle was one of only a handful of Canadians quoted in the book—in company with Pierre and Margaret Trudeau—and the only cat!" says Bobbi with pride.

By the time Simon was 10 years old he was writing a regular column for the *West Quebec Post*, as well as columns for the Canadian children's magazine *JAM* and the American national newsletter *PURRRRR!* Bobbi was being paid for all of them. He had a publicity mug shot next to his columns and became known as "The Classy Cat in the Black Fur Tuxedo."

Then, at the height of his fame, the unthinkable happened: Simon Teakettle lived the last of his nine lives. Despite her resolution years ago to never grieve for a cat again, Bobbi missed Simon dreadfully. He was more than a friend and partner; he was a Name. He had responsibilities. He had a readership that adored him. A media tour was in the offing. She couldn't let them down. Bobbi knew what she had to do.

Simon Teakettle, she decided, must go on. And that meant she had to once more take a chance with her affection. This time she knew there would be no holding back. "I went to the SPCA," she relates, "and told them I needed a kitten to match this mug shot." Simon Teakettle was a long-time supporter of the SPCA, and everyone there knew of him, so they were most helpful. But as luck would have it, there was an unexpected shortage of black kittens that spring. There were orange kittens, grey kittens, calico kittens and tabby kittens, but no handsome all-black kittens. Then a feral cat was brought in with her litter of five—a tabby, a spotted black and white and three black kittens.

Feral kittens can have a hard time adjusting to domesticity, and Bobbi wasn't sure this would work. The mother was essentially wild. The other kittens scratched and scrambled to get away from her. Then she picked up one, a little black male with a tiny locket of white at his throat. "He sat in the palm of my hand and just looked at me. And I knew. This was the one." The shelter workers were skeptical, but Bobbi's certainty convinced them. Simon Teakettle the Younger, known as Tiki, went home with Bobbi. A new chapter in the Simon Teakettle saga began.

From early kittenhood, Simon Teakettle the Younger showed unusual interest in everything human. "Although he was born in a barn to a feral mother with grey tabby markings, he appears to have a significant portion of Siamese genes," says Bobbi. "He is vocal, smart and uses his paw like many Siamese do. He's also very Siamese in his body type: lean and compact with a narrow face."

Since Bobbi knew Tiki would have to face the spotlights, she decided to put these personality traits to good use: she trained him. "He responds to many commands including

come, stay, sit, give me your paw, sit up, catch it and get down."
But why stop there? Tiki also understands more complex
questions, such as: Do you want to go on the front porch or in
the backyard? (He responds by going to the door he prefers.)
Would you like a fresh drink? (He goes into the bathroom,
jumps on the counter where his water bowl is and lifts his
paw.) Where's your bear? (He finds his teddy bear.)

"I have also taught him the concept of ball," adds
Bobbi. "He knows the word means anything in the shape
of a ball, regardless of its size, colour or composition."
When she asks him to "touch the ball" and identify it in an
assortment of other items, he can do it, whether the ball in
question is a sparkly, fuzzy green ball, a small yellow plush
ball, a large patchwork plastic ball or a purple rubber ball
with a bell inside.

"He has quite a repertoire now," Bobbi says proudly.
"I try to teach him a new behaviour every year." He even
knows when he's been naughty. "The other day I told him,
'You better take a nap.' Off he trotted, right away." She
smiles, remembering. "I'd sent him to his room!"

Bobbi also insisted Tiki learn to appreciate the local
wildlife as 'paws-off' entertainment, rather than as snacks.
"He's learned not to chase the birds," she says. "He knows
that if he chases them, they fly away and don't come back.
So he lies quietly in the foliage and watches."

He and the squirrels have even devised an elaborate
game. Tiki sits and watches them, and when they start to

run he gives them a head start. They scamper up the tree, he stretches full-length against the tree trunk, then he goes back to wait for them to come down so the game can start again. "When the babies first descend from the tree, they're not afraid of him," says Bobbi. "He's extremely respectful of them because they don't know the rules yet. So he'll just sit six or eight feet away, quiet as can be, watching them eat their seeds."

Teaching a cat *not* to hunt isn't difficult, but it takes a great deal of patience. "I'd go outside with him on a leash," Bobbi explains. "Whenever he made predatory body postures or noises, I'd scold him and pull him back. Sometimes I'd go out and sit with him, wait for a bird or squirrel to appear, then hold him on my lap and encourage him to sit quietly and watch. He is really smart."

In fact, he's decided that if he can't chase the birds, no one else can either. "He actually keeps other neighbourhood cats away from 'his' birds. These are pets, friends—not food. Of course," adds Bobbi, "I'd never let a cat outside when he's hungry. I always tell him to finish his breakfast first."

Although Simon the Younger is a very different cat from Simon the Elder, the public persona has remained consistent. Words continue to appear under his picture and Simon Teakettle has kept his loyal followers happy. Bobbi reports that she and Simon Teakettle are currently waging an anthology war. "We're published in 21 anthologies altogether. He's in 4; I'm in 17." Their award-winning book

Mewsings/Musings contains humorous essays by Bobbi as well as a compilation of the best-loved pieces of both Simon the Elder and Simon the Younger.

Tiki is now 16 years old, a healthy, active bundle of energy. But Bobbi knows she has to cherish each day with him. Sharing her career with her cats has brought Bobbi far more than professional success. "I've always said that one of my problems is that I write for work and I write as a hobby," she says. "I really think I have learned a lot about tapping my own creativity by adopting a totally different persona." Of course, inspiration is nurtured by all of the senses, including touch. The act of petting an animal is known to have a calming effect on the body, while stimulating the creativity centres in the right side of the brain. It's hard not to smile when you're with a cat, a benefit that can sometimes be distracting. "For my very serious writing I sometimes have to wait till he's napping," Bobbi wryly confesses.

In spite of the fact that Barbara Florio Graham is a professional journalist with three books to her credit, she knows the real score. The Simon Teakettles, both the Elder and the Younger, have earned their own cat food and kitty litter from the get-go. "This is my business, but I work for him," she states matter-of-factly. "After all, I open the food. I clean the litter box."

CHAPTER

4

Prescription Pets:
Cats Who Heal

"There are two means of refuge from the miseries of life: music and cats." —ALBERT SCHWEITZER

IN 1994, AL HODGKINSON SAT in the doctor's office reeling from the news he'd just been given. "Put your affairs in order," the doctor said. "You have terminal prostate cancer." Al did have the option of trying radiation therapy in the hope that it might extend his life for one more year, but he was told not to expect anything more.

Al and his wife Pat looked at each other and knew they had to try everything possible, no matter how unlikely. Thirty-five radiation treatments later, Al wondered if his last year of life would be worth living. He returned home in a wheelchair, barely able to move his legs.

In spite of the bleak prognosis Al had been given, the radiation treatment was successful; his cancer was defeated. The treatments themselves, however, resulted in nerve damage that left him with sensory deficits, mobility problems and pain. "Until a couple of months ago, a shower was my only means of bathing," he explains. "When sitting in a tub, I could not establish whether the water temperature was hot or cold." But it was the pain that made him wonder whether the cure was worse than the disease. When the throbbing struck, even powerful analgesics didn't last long enough to control agony so intense that sometimes all Al could do was count the minutes, tears rolling down his face, until he could take another painkiller.

One night while Al and Pat were watching television, the pain was especially severe. Pat sat beside him helplessly as he struggled to contain his misery until it was time for his next pill. "About 20 minutes later," Al recalls, "Pat asked me if the pain had stopped." He realized he was no longer crying, and the pain had indeed subsided. "She asked me to look at what was sitting on my lap . . . and purring." It was their cat, Precious.

Precious, an orphan from birth, was the only one of her litter to survive. In 1993, when her first home with Al and Pat's daughter didn't work out due to allergies, Al volunteered to take her back to the shelter. They made a brief stop at home first, and within minutes Precious had endeared herself to both of them. The shelter was forgotten, and Precious has been with the Hodgkinsons ever since.

Al and Pat began to notice that Precious exhibited certain

behaviours only when Al's pain was at its worst. She seemed to know when the pain reached its peak, and at that point she'd leap onto Al's lap and start purring. Of course, she'd hop up onto his lap at other times as well, but her manner was different at those times, and she didn't purr. It was as if she was acutely aware of Al's emotions and recognized his painful episodes as the times when he needed her talents the most. "We started to realize that this had been happening for quite a while, even if we didn't understand why or how," says Al. One theory is that the sound waves of the feline purr are in the same range as the ultrasound used to manage pain disorders. "Gee," Al jokes, "I have my own free ultrasound machine—and it comes with a fur coat!"

Some of his medical caregivers are skeptical, but none of them can deny the improvement in Al's health. Most significantly, he has long surpassed the one-year extension that the radiation therapy was supposed to give him. "I've progressed from a wheelchair to two canes to one cane. Three years ago, I went to no canes at all. And," adds Al, "today and for the past six years, I take no prescription medication at all. If and when pain strikes, Precious seems to know, and when she comes . . . pain runs away."

Al still has pain from time to time, but the intensity and frequency are now within tolerable levels—and if they get out of hand, Precious always hops up into his lap to provide her special therapy.

* * *

Experiences like Al's provide the foundation for animal-assisted therapy, or pet visitation. Retired nurse Sadey Guy of Sidney, BC, knows that animals can play a role alongside modern medicine to promote healing; she's been immersed in both all her life. Born in Wales to parents who were master and matron of an English hospital, Sadey literally grew up surrounded by patients. As a child, she often visited the wards, sometimes bringing her rabbits or other pets along. It was a comfortable environment for her, but she never intended to be a nurse herself. "No, Mom," she remembers telling her mother, "I like people. I can't stick needles into them."

Famous last words! Sadey Guy became a nurse after all and loved her work. When it came time to retire, she couldn't imagine leaving the hospital setting permanently. Then she had an idea. In her last few years of nursing, she'd been working with elderly patients in extended care. Sadey had witnessed wonderful relationships spring up between patients and resident pets. "It was the natural thing to do in those days," she says. "In the 70s, when animal therapy first began to catch on, animals weren't often allowed in acute-care hospitals, but they were welcomed into extended-care facilities." Aquarium fish and birds were often permanent residents, but at that time even cats and dogs began to be welcomed into hospitals.

Toby, a collie-cross who lived in the extended-care facility where Sadey worked, took his job very seriously. He sat near various patients in turn, allowing them to pet him and talk to him. Toby seemed to be aware of the people whose emotional needs he could fill and gravitated toward them. Then, while outside one day, Toby was hit by a car and badly injured. He recovered, but he was never the same. A staff member adopted him, and Toby continued to visit residents, but he wasn't able to live among them anymore. "I started to think it was too much for the dogs," says Sadey. "Cats love people, but they'll excuse themselves when it's time for a break. Dogs will stay by their people forever. Dogs can get worn out."

Sadey had wanted to bring animals and patients together but wasn't sure how she should go about it. "When I retired in 1988, just after Toby's accident, I thought, 'That's what I should do!'" Sadey had already made many hospital visits with Duchess, her aging Welsh corgi, and her black cat, Tiger. She wanted to do more.

She contacted the local Society for the Prevention of Cruelty to Animals (SPCA), because she knew the inspectors already did occasional hospital visits with dogs or cats awaiting adoption. Maybe, she thought, they would lend some of their pets out for visitation purposes. But she quickly realized that wasn't a solution. The SPCA naturally wanted their animals to be adopted, not borrowed. And patients didn't want to have to get to know a strange animal each visit. Sadey's idea was growing, but it needed structure. She continued to look for people to help her and eventually connected with Volunteer Victoria, an association that works to help volunteer groups. There, Sadey's idea gathered momentum. With the help of Volunteer Victoria, the group she envisioned became an official, registered non-profit association. The Pacific Animal Therapy Society was born. When it was time for P.A.T.S. Pets, as the group is called, to find a mascot, Sadey knew exactly who it would be. Toby, who lived until the distinguished age of 17, perfectly symbolized Sadey's vision. "We adopted Toby as our logo for P.A.T.S. Pets," says Sadey, "so he lives on in love."

Knowing health care as she does, Sadey solicited the input of medical administration, tailoring the program to best meet the specific requirements of hospitals, retirement homes and other facilities in which residents could benefit from interaction with animals. "We talked to the volunteer coordinators at the big hospitals," she says, "and asked them what they wanted from us."

Most visits are on an individual basis and usually last for about an hour. While the majority of animal visitors are dogs, P.A.T.S. therapy pets include cats, rabbits, birds, goats and even more unusual guests such as a llama, a miniature horse and a snake. "We've found that bonding forms with certain folk and all three—the pet, the owner and the patient— receive blessings through this friendship," says Sadey.

Human volunteers receive orientation regarding safety procedures, confidentiality and other issues relevant to the facilities they visit. Throughout the year, volunteers have the opportunity to attend workshops presented by health care professionals and receive special training in listening and support skills. They even work on a rotating schedule to ensure that this public service is available every day of the year. "Sometimes people go to a specific hospital once a week for regularly scheduled visits," says Sadey. "Other times we go as a group."

Most volunteers have one pet that they use for visitation; a few alternate between more than one. But each pet is carefully evaluated before being allowed into the program. The requirements are strict: they must be in good health, fully vaccinated and temperamentally suitable. They must be comfortable in strange surroundings, and they must not panic at strange noises or rough contact. Dogs must have basic obedience. Cats must come when called. "In a hospital basins get dropped, carts clatter and clang," explains Sadey. "Alzheimer's patients might pull an ear or tail without knowing, or a spastic person might accidentally knock into the animals when they reach out." Of course, Sadey adds, to protect fragile skin, pets' nails must be kept trimmed.

It's not a job description that fits a lot of felines. Strangers and loud noises are bad enough, let alone a weekly manicure! But Sadey doesn't waver on her rules. "You want a cat that will look around to see what's happening, but not bolt." Sadey knew that the right cats could make great therapy pets.

The first cat to fit the bill was a big, beautiful, silver-tipped Persian named Sylvia Serina. Her owner had fostered many stray animals over the years, so Sylvia was accustomed to lots of different faces coming and going. Sadey hoped this accepting attitude would carry over to the patients she'd meet on the ward, and it did. For over three years, until she and her owner moved, Sylvia Serina spent countless hours purring quietly on the laps of her bedridden friends, comforting them with her warmth. "I think the purring helps folks realize how content and happy they are to be with them," says Sadey.

Then there was Duke, an ordinary ginger shorthair who loved to be where the action was. "Nothing worried him," says Sadey. "He'd sit in a lap or wander around. You could take him in to visit children as well as adults." In fact, the children were his biggest fans. During his time in the program, Duke worked his way through almost every hospital department, including the surgical and rehabilitation wards where many of the kids he visited were in for lengthy stays. Duke quickly became a favourite among them. Then, to the sorrow of his many friends, Duke suddenly died. Visitation days weren't quite so special anymore.

His owner, Diane Taylor, wanted to continue what Duke had started, so she went to the local SPCA, hoping to find another cat to fill the void. She came home with Simon. At 17 pounds of pure muscle, he was a beautiful, powerful cat. But would he have the right personality? Duke was a hard act to follow. "We weren't sure how he would do," recalls Sadey. "We waited awhile before testing him." Time, they hoped, would help Simon adjust to his new life enough to be comfortable meeting new people. Then one day Simon was ready. They introduced him to a patient who had just finished her lunch. He sat down on the bed beside her, and when she offered him her leftover milk, he politely accepted.

When Simon realized the rewards of being a hospital visitor, he threw himself into the role with great enthusiasm. And, like his predecessor, he's learned to love children. At a visit to a preschool class, Simon makes himself right at home, sitting at a low table among the students. If he's in the right mood, he offers them his paw, much to their delight. "Simon is coming along just fine," says Sadey. "He's become so much like Duke."

Sadey knows that not everyone likes cats. In fact, sometimes she'll be told that a certain patient doesn't want a visit from *any* of the animals. She understands and doesn't let it bother her, because more often the response is just the opposite. "Just as many say, 'No dogs, but I love cats!'" she comments. "Some people get very emotional. They hold their arms out, calling, 'Bring him here, bring him here. Leave him here!'"

That emotional reaction touches a chord with Sadey. She doesn't have a cat now, but hopes to have one again soon. "I miss my cat terribly," she admits. Until the right cat comes along, she keeps busy with her dog, a Welsh terrier named Dylan Thomas, who has seemingly unlimited energy and enthusiasm. "He is wonderful," says Sadey. "A very feeling creature. He helps many folks—including me."

Joy, like illness, can be contagious. Happiness, like medicine, can heal. Whenever a cheery visit from an animal lifts the spirits of someone sick or in pain, Sadey knows her work has been worthwhile. People like Al Hodgkinson simply reaffirm her belief that pets affect our health in far more ways than we understand. It's the kind of story that keeps the volunteers at P.A.T.S. going back, even when their contributions come at an emotional cost. Every time they look for an old friend only to find an empty bed, they are reminded that each visit could be the last. "Still," says Sadey, "we would not change our volunteering experience. We love it, and its rewards are unbelievable."

The rewards took on a tangible form recently when Sadey Guy received the Valued Elder Recognition Award, sponsored by the University of Victoria Centre on Aging. A tree with a plaque honouring Sadey's contribution to humanity, society and community now grows on the university grounds. What started as a bridge between Sadey's professional life and her retirement has grown into something much larger. Sharing the healing power of pets through P.A.T.S. reminds people—volunteers and patients alike—that life is good. "There's a world outside," says Sadey, "that's worth getting better for."

5

Miracle Babies

"Where there is great love there are always miracles."
—WILLA CATHER

CAROLINE CAMERON AND NANCY HUTCHINSON knew that if they were going to breed cats, they had to do it right. That meant running it as a business and treating their cats as the valuable assets they were. So the two friends turned their London, Ontario, home into the Katzanova Himalayan Cattery, breeding champion Himalayan cats—registered, health-guaranteed and fully socialized. They quickly established a firm reputation in the competitive world of cat shows as breeders of quality, well-nurtured kittens. But behind the ambition, Caroline had a secret wish. "I wanted a sealpoint as a pet," she confesses. "As breeders we weren't keeping any Himmies as pets. When you're a breeder you are supposed to think with your head, not your heart."

But Himalayans are a breed that appeals to the heart. They are the result of an attempt to create a Persian-Siamese cross, an idea that proved more difficult to realize than breeders expected. The goal was to obtain a cat that combined the compact, stocky ("cobby") body and long, luxurious coat of a Persian with the colour points and blue eyes of the Siamese. Many litters were bred in which kittens that had one trait didn't have the other. Finally breeders found success, and in 1950 the Himalayan breed was born. They are now one of the most popular pedigreed felines in the cat fancy, that elite group of cat lovers dedicated to refining their chosen breeds. Sealpoint Himalayans, perhaps the best-known colour variety, are truly stunning: snub-nosed faces, deep blue eyes and long, beige body fur tipped with rich, dark brown fur on the ears, mask, paws and tail. But as beautiful as these cats are, it's their personality that appeals to people. "Himalayans are similar to a Persian but with much more of a spark," says Caroline. "They love to follow you around like a puppy dog!"

Caroline and Nancy loved their cats and were committed to spending whatever time, energy and money was necessary to improve the breed. Caroline explains, "Breeding is not a big money-maker. We wanted to jump in with both feet and do it properly. If you do it right, that means registering every litter with the Canadian Cat Association and keeping very tight records: every vaccination, every time we used antibiotics, it all had to be accounted for. All the adult cats had to be tested for polycystic kidney disease, feline leukemia and feline immunodeficiency virus."

So Caroline set her dream to one side and continued with the practical work of running a cattery. And there was a lot of it. "I quit my job to be home with these guys," she says. "I had to clean litter boxes three times a day and scrub the floors with bleach and water. To maximize efficiency and ensure the well-being of the cats, Caroline and Nancy aimed to have two males and eight to ten females in their cattery. At one time, Katzanova had 12 adults and 18 kittens, but they were definitely prepared; each room in the house had a different purpose. "One room was for mating only; the males lived there full-time," says Caroline. "We had one room as a nursery only and one room for females that don't get along with other females. Fortunately, we only had a couple like that. The others got along fantastically well, especially considering the number of cats we had."

After two years in the business, they'd acquired a wealth of experience. They'd learned how to evaluate kittens shortly after birth to decide which would be raised for showing, which should be kept for breeding and which ones would be sold as pets. So when Caroline was looking over one particular litter, she knew there was one especially good one in it. "He looked like he'd make a good breeder," she recalls, "possibly even a show cat." But they'd also learned that the breed could be somewhat delicate. When she found that this young hopeful's eyes had both opened when it was only three days old, her heart dropped; kittens' eyes don't usually open until around 10 to 14 days of age. "They were closed again by the next morning, but it was just long enough for an infection to start."

"Off to the veterinarian I went with this tiny newborn. I got ointment and medication to clear up the infection," says Caroline. "The vet instructed me to clean the kitten's eyes several times a day, and showed me how to do it, and I did exactly that." But while cleaning the area one day, it became all too obvious that she was losing the battle. As she moved the swab gently across his tiny face, she was horrified to see what looked like part of the eye dissolve onto the cotton ball.

The veterinarian confirmed her fears. The eye was gone, but there was still worse news. The infection that destroyed the eye was threatening to overwhelm the tiny body. Even with round-the-clock care, the vet warned, the kitten had little chance of survival. He was too small and too young to cope with such an assault on the system. In every way, the odds were against him.

But for Caroline, the smallest chance was enough to keep her fighting. She kept him in a box beside her at all times, with a heating pad and baby receiving blankets to keep him warm. Hour after hour she treated him with various remedies: tiny amounts of medication, antibiotic drops and fluids by mouth, but there was little response.

It was touch and go. At one point the veterinarian advised Caroline to prepare to lose him. But she kept hoping for a miracle. Throughout the night, she kept up her ministrations, reminding him that she was there and that he should keep fighting. Morning came with no change, but still she continued. He wasn't getting better, but nor was he getting worse; that was enough reason to keep trying.

Then, in the microscopic battle waging within the tiny body, the tide turned. Caroline's hopes surged as she saw the kitten make a few feeble movements. "Within 24 to 48 hours I noticed an improvement in him," she recalls. "He started crawling on his tummy and showing a few livelier signs." Because he was too weak to nurse, Caroline had been feeding him with an eyedropper, giving him formula specially designed to replace mother cat's milk. Hour by hour, day by day, she watched him as he fed. It wasn't just her imagination. He was definitely improving. "Once he looked stronger," says Caroline, "I put him back with his mother, and he started nursing again." This was a hurdle. Could he compete with his littermates and get the nourishment he needed?

Apparently he could; he continued to grow and gain weight. Then his other eye opened up. This was the sticking point. A cat with one blind eye can live a normal life; helping a cat cope with complete blindness would be a huge challenge. But to Caroline's relief the eye was normal. "The veterinarian checked it and said it was all fine. The minute I knew he was going to make it, I said, 'Nancy, I've got to keep him!'"

And so the Katzanova Cattery had its very first pet Himmie. Himalayan kittens are born completely white, so Caroline endured several weeks of suspense wondering what colour he would be. To her delight, this kitten turned out to be the handsome sealpoint she had secretly wanted for years. He was to become her pride and joy, never to be bred, sold or shown—a cat just for her. Patch Adams, as she named him, had survived against all odds, and she couldn't let him go.

"Once Patch fully recovered, he was a real delight. What is so neat about the Himalayan is that they love the human touch, and they like to be wherever you are. They will follow you from room to room, all around the house." As Patch has regained his strength and continues to grow, he follows Caroline everywhere. He sits at the stairs watching her when she goes out, and when she returns he runs to greet her.

Patch is very much a hands-on cat, accustomed to being toted around in Caroline's arms and curling up in her lap for a cuddle whenever she sits down. "Patch became my new best friend, my buddy, the love of my life," says Caroline. "He's the sealpoint Himmie I had so desperately wanted."

No matter how much they are cherished, most cattery cats eventually end up somewhere other than where they started. Kittens are born and raised for the specific purpose of being sold to loving homes. Retired breeding cats are placed with people who want adults rather than youngsters. Caroline and Nancy have said goodbye to many much-loved cats over the years, but one cat in particular, Patch Adams, Caroline's One-Eyed Jack, isn't going anywhere.

Miracle Babies

* * *

Birman breeder Betty Sleep of Coles Island, New Brunswick, knows the rich history behind her chosen breed. According to ancient legend in Burma (Myanmar), a white temple cat named Sinh sat on the chest of the dying priest Mun-ha, before the statues of the goddess. When the holy man died, the cat was transformed. His feet remained white like the priest's beard, but his head, tail and legs turned a rich brown, the colour of the earth, and his eyes took on the goddess statue's deep blue glance. Today, the "Sacred Cat of Burma" is known as the Birman. Not to be confused with either the Himalayan or the Burmese, the Birman is an intelligent, gentle breed distinguished by pure white gloves on all four feet.

But romance and glamour aside, to breed and show champion Birman cats is a demanding occupation. Betty was just catching her breath after hand-rearing an orphan kitten and was anticipating a nice, quiet season in the cattery. Late one evening in August 2002, however, she realized it was not to be. Betty was finishing up some paperwork at her computer when she noticed one of her pregnant females acting suspiciously. This cat wasn't due to give birth for nearly a week, so Betty was shocked when she found what looked like a kitten's head emerging from the mother. She grabbed her delivery supplies and took the cat to the birthing box. "Once there," she says, "I discovered it was an 'old' placenta." The placenta, which links mother and baby together before birth, had detached from the uterus; without a healthy placenta, there's no way for the baby to get vital nutrients, including oxygen. X-rays had revealed earlier that three kittens would be born. Now only two would be born alive.

Hoping to save the remaining kittens, Betty rushed the mother cat to her veterinarian. She suspected a Caesarean section was the only chance for the remaining kittens, even though they weren't ready to be born yet. But either way it was risky. Cats have a normal gestation period of 63 days; even a couple of days can make the difference between full-term and premature babies. At Day 58, these kittens were scraping the edge of viability. "If you have a dead kitten," explains Betty, "chances are it will decompose, and not necessarily quickly. By the time you realize it's decomposing, your queen [the mother cat] may be compromised and your other kittens dead." There was no choice. The kittens would have to be delivered surgically.

By the time she reached the clinic, it was past midnight. The veterinary team set to work, preparing to perform a Caesarean section. Soon the first kitten, a perfectly formed male, was born. But he wasn't breathing and his skin was white, suggesting blood circulation had stopped some time ago. "I could pretty much tell by looking that he had been dead for several hours," says Betty. "He had no reflexes, no reactions, nothing."

Still, you never know. Betty massaged and stimulated the little body, hoping against hope that she was wrong and this kitten might still live. Rubbing and massaging them this way mimics the mother cat's rough licking and helps stimulate their respiratory system. "I was still working on the first one when the vet came out of the operating room," recalls Betty. "He had his hands cupped. I looked inside, and he held what looked like a little purple grape. We just sort of stood there and stared at it." She passed the first kitten to someone else and laid this tiny one out on the towels to start resuscitation efforts. In a kitten of normal size, Betty would put a square of gauze over the muzzle before blowing into it to stimulate respiration. But a two-inch square of gauze was bigger than this little speck's entire body. Betty did the best she could, encouraging the heartbeat by tapping the wee chest and puffing softly into the tiny nostrils from time to time. Slowly the kitten's skin began to lose its dusky purple tinge. From the operating room, Betty could hear the veterinarian yelling at her to keep going. Suddenly the kitten's body shuddered, and the tiny female began to breathe.

Newborn kittens are very susceptible to heat loss, so during her efforts Betty kept the infant on a terry-cloth covered hot-water bottle. "A towel was too big to use on her," recalls Betty, "so I used the corner of a face cloth." After about 15 minutes, enough vital oxygen reached the kitten's tissues to turn her skin a more normal pinkish colour. Finally Betty was able to take a break, pull back the cloth and examine her properly. The relief of getting her breathing quickly faded. "It was like looking at a baby bird that had fallen out of its nest," she says. "She had those big dark eyes that have hardly any tissue over them. She had some hair on the top of her head and down her back, but the skin on her abdomen was so transparent you could almost see her organs." She was such a wisp that the scale wouldn't even register a weight. They guessed she weighed maybe 28 grams or one ounce, about the size of a Cadbury Easter Cream Egg. This baby was less than a third of the size of a normal kitten.

While Betty absorbed the reality of this kitten's fragile hold on life, she heard a squeaking sound from the operating room. One kitten at least, another female, was born healthy and energetic. But Betty knew the chances were slim that she'd still have two kittens in the morning.

To her surprise, both kittens lived through the night, and Betty took all three cats home. Unfortunately, the mother cat refused to have anything to do with her new family. The premature delivery meant she didn't yet have the hormone levels that trigger the feline mothering instinct. Betty forced her to lie down with the kittens, hoping they'd get a bit of colostrum, the early milk rich in antibodies. But as soon as she was allowed, the mother cat leaped away from her babies. Betty kept hoping the mother would come around, but even with drug therapy she simply had no milk. After four days she had to admit it was a lost cause. Betty, with her feeding syringes, was the best mom these kittens would be getting.

Then one night, during a midnight feeding, Betty noticed the healthy kitten wasn't as vigorous as she'd been earlier. Knowing how quickly kittens can fade, she immediately paged her veterinarian. But even before the call had been returned, the kitten died. "We were down to the grape," says Betty. Still, one was better than none. Betty determined to do everything she could to keep this last baby alive. She made her a little nest in a carrier with a heating pad and a sheepskin covering. She put the carrier next to her on the bed, and for the next several weeks, Betty barely let the kitten out of her sight.

"I was afraid to name her," admits Betty. But the kitten had to be called something. By the alphabetical naming tradition followed by the cat fancy in North America, 2002 was year "Z." Then it hit her—the perfect "Z" name for a kitten who had resembled a grape at birth—Zinfandel. The unlikely survivor now had a handle. Betty and the kitten, dubbed Fan, settled into a routine of sorts, but it was still difficult to believe this little Zinfandel might actually survive. "The only way I could lift her was to take my thumb and forefinger and gently pick her up by the barest flap of skin," says Betty. "Touching her was like touching a rubber glove. Even at two weeks she was just starting to look like a newborn kitten. I've never seen anything like it before and never want to see anything like it again. It's the smallest thing I've ever seen survive." The rule of thumb for feeding orphan kittens, according to Betty, is 24 millilitres of formula for every 100 grams of body weight. At that time, Fan was getting about six millilitres, just over a teaspoon, in a 24-hour period.

Betty hated to see Fan all alone. Cats rarely give birth to single kittens; this one had neither littermates nor a mother to keep her warm and cosy. So when Fan was about 10 days old, Betty got her a soft, terry-cloth–covered beanbag toy with "It's a Girl!" written on it. Fan quickly learned to crawl underneath this toy, sandwiching herself between the warm pad below and the warmth reflected from above.

Then at three weeks, disaster struck. Artificial formula, while as good as science can make it, isn't mother cat's milk, and hand-reared kittens often have difficulty digesting it properly. Fan became severely constipated, a situation that could develop into a serious condition known as megacolon, where the bowel is permanently overstretched. For five days, Betty and the vet tried everything: more water, laxatives, corn syrup and even enemas. Finally, though she was less than a month of age and weighed a mere seven ounces, they decided to try one last-ditch effort and put the kitten on solid foods. Amazingly, Fan's condition began to improve. Syringe-fed kitten food pureed with warm water eventually remedied the problem.

They weren't over the hump yet. Lack of sleep was beginning to take its toll on Betty. She began to wonder how much longer she could carry on without becoming ill herself. Between feedings she caught what sleep she could, propped upright with Fan's carrier next to her on the bed. But two weeks later, in the wee hours of the morning, Fan began vomiting. It would be another night without rest for Betty.

"At that age—Fan was 31 days old—a kitten can dehydrate and die in a couple of hours," says Betty. And at 225 grams, Fan was still less than half the weight of a normal kitten the same age. She couldn't afford to lose even a gram.

By six o'clock in the morning, Betty was at the veterinary clinic again. After a few hours of treatment with fluids and medication, Fan's vomiting stopped. Although the diarrhea continued throughout the day, the miniscule kitten looked like she was getting better. Betty took Fan home and hoped she'd continue to improve. "I put her back in her carrier and she crawled under her beanie, turned her back and went to sleep." Betty lay back against the headboard and tried to relax, but sleep eluded her. Finally, at about four o'clock the next morning, she decided to feed Fan even though it wasn't quite time yet. "I reached in to pick her up and almost had a heart attack," recalls Betty. "She didn't move. Although she was breathing and her eyes were open, she was unresponsive. Her eyes were even starting to dry." At some point during the night, Fan had crossed the line between sleep and unconsciousness, and by sunrise, for the second time in two days, Betty and Fan were at the veterinary hospital.

"That morning was an absolute circus," says Betty. "We filled her with subcutaneous fluids until she looked like a water balloon." Dextrose and electrolyte solutions were put by tube into her stomach. There was no explanation for her sudden stupor and little hope she'd come out of it, but as long as the kitten kept breathing, Betty determined to keep trying. It didn't seem to matter what they did, Fan lay motionless, barely alive. Finally the veterinarian left to prepare for the regular workday. Betty continued, begging the weak little mite not to give up. For a long time nothing changed. Then, within a few moments, Fan twitched and seemed to regain consciousness. She couldn't stand up or even raise her head, but she was definitely awake. Within a short time, the bloated kitten rolled over, her body sloshing with all the liquids that had been injected into her. When the veterinarian returned 30 minutes later, he was just in time to see Fan get up, stagger across the blanket and nip Betty weakly on the hand in greeting. "I wish I'd had a camera!" Betty chuckles at the memory of his amazement. "That vet just stood there and stared at her. He picked her up, checked her over and then just shook his head." Neither of them had ever seen anything so close to death come back to life.

To this day they don't know what caused Fan's near-fatal illness. But after that episode, the road slowly evened out and she matured into a beautiful cat. When Fan was seven months of age, Betty showed her for the first and last time. "She took six finals in ten rings and wound up as fourth-best all-breed kitten in the Eastern Canada region of the American Cat Fanciers Association," says Betty proudly. "She was perfectly marked, as Birmans go, with very good body structure."

Eventually Betty had to decide what to do with Fan. In spite of the Birman's success, Betty didn't feel Fan enjoyed being a show cat. Should she keep her as a pet? "I hung onto her because I was almost afraid to let her go," admits Betty. "That little heartstring—you can only stretch it so far!" She hadn't let anyone know that Fan was available, but then an inquiry came from a couple she knew. They'd bought a kitten from Betty earlier, a full sister of Fan's from one of Fan's mother's subsequent litters. They desperately wanted a companion for this cat and were disappointed to learn that all Betty's kittens were already spoken for. But when they heard about Fan they wanted her immediately. "There are times when people ask for a cat and you know they're going to give it a good home," says Betty. "I thought this was where Fan was meant to go."

As a breeder, Betty knows that not all kittens can be saved. But when she's presented with a kitten fighting for life, she doesn't only think like a breeder. "I can't set it aside to die naturally," she says. "If it's trying that hard to live, it's my responsibility to give it every possible chance." It's a triumph of the will to live.

And for Betty, it's bearing witness to a miracle.

6

The Cat Man
of Parliament Hill

*"You will always be lucky if you know how to make friends
with strange cats."* —COLONIAL AMERICAN PROVERB

IT'S A GREY DAY. Scudding clouds reflect off the surface of the
Ottawa River behind the black silhouettes of leafless trees.
Lunchtime office crowds, dodging slower-paced tourists
and canoodling lovers, scurry along the concrete walkways
that wind in a ribbon between stony-faced buildings. Past
the Queen Victoria statue, to the left of the central building,
tourists pause. Behind the wrought-iron fence, a cluster of
ramshackle but sturdy hutches, wooden chairs and pet-food
dishes attract their attention. They appear out of place in the
midst of the stately Victorian- and Gothic Revival–styled
Parliament Buildings, but these little shelters have become
an institution in their own right.

Cats live in these shelters, but they aren't the only

animals to take protection from the elements here. Squirrels nibble the crumbs left in the dishes, and a fat groundhog scuttles beneath the boardwalk. In the branches overhead, sparrows huddle together and pigeons ruffle their feathers impatiently. The creatures seem to wait in a hush of expectancy. Local employees hurry inattentively back to their offices as the lunch hour comes to an end—this peculiar gathering is nothing new to them—but visitors peer through the bars of the fence, curious about the wildlife-tolerant cats hovering nearby.

Then the air is filled with the majestic peal of the Peace Tower clock chiming one o'clock. As if on cue, more cats—many of whom spend their days largely hidden from view—begin to emerge from their secret haunts. Tourists scramble for their cameras.

A big orange and white male pads delicately up to the fence and sits gracefully. A fluffy grey tabby leaps down from a branch. An old calico yawns and stretches out from inside her wooden shelter. From nooks and crannies, high and low, they materialize. And they are not disappointed. It's lunchtime and René Chartrand, the Cat Man, has arrived.

Once upon a time, the plateau now known as Parliament Hill housed troops of soldiers and was called Barracks Hill. In the mid-1800s, the plateau became the location of the nation's government, which was housed in three buildings referred to as West Block, East Block and Centre Block. Centre Block was destroyed by fire in 1916 and subsequently rebuilt, but the other two still stand as originally constructed. Today they hold the offices of senators and Members of Parliament, as well as the House of Commons and the Senate itself. In addition to the more public figures, vast numbers of support personnel—aides, clerical workers, maintenance staff and others—go about their duties. The politically ambitious can always be seen scurrying one way or another. But back when the buildings were first constructed, other creatures were scurrying besides upwardly mobile assistants. Parliament Hill had a serious rodent problem.

As far back as 1877, according to popular local history, cats were brought in to deal with the burgeoning vermin population on the Hill. These cats did their jobs, faithfully keeping mice and rats in check throughout the many buildings. They stayed out of the way and raised their offspring to do the same. In time, a colony of semi-domesticated cats was established on Parliament Hill. They belonged to no one and answered to no one.

But the cats did their job too well; as rodents became less of a problem, the cats on the Hill could no longer rely on their hunting skills to stay fed. The colony had turned into a shifting, growing group of homeless stray cats—hungry, wild and desperately in need of someone to care for them. Since legend has it that this colony is made up of descendants of the mousers that once worked in Her Majesty's service, many people felt they deserved better.

René Chartrand. ROXANNE WILLEMS SNOPEK

In the late 1970s, a compassionate cat lover named Irene Desormeaux decided it was time to do something about it. They didn't need much—a little protection from the weather and a bit of food. So she had two little wooden shelters built, each large enough to house up to 20 cats. Round openings allowed easy access for the occupants, as well as contributing a whimsical appeal to the shelters. The houses were built to protect the cats from the elements. Waterproof shingles made for a dry roof, and a wide overhang kept wind and snow from getting in. During the coldest months, they were filled with straw for additional insulation.

But caring for a couple dozen cats was a great deal of work for this elderly woman. When her health began to decline, she enlisted the help of her friend and neighbour, René Chartrand. In 1987, on her deathbed, Irene begged René to take care of the cats for her. He promised her he would look after them until another permanent caretaker could be found. He's done it ever since. Now people call him the Cat Man of Parliament Hill. It's a natural part of his life. "There have been cats there since I was a little boy, and now I'm 83. We used to go there and look for litters of kittens," recalls René.

Today there are 28 felines residing on the Hill. Every day, no matter what the weather, René gets on the bus, travels across town and trudges up to the shelter with his bag of supplies. Every day the menagerie greets him with an assortment of welcomes: throaty purrs, waving tails and the occasional wash with a rough tongue. They seem to understand the depth of René's commitment to their well-being. He sets down his battered backpack and begins to pull out the day's feast. A few dishes go here, some go there and one gets tucked into the corner where the shy cat hides out. Kibble goes into the metal dishes, at least eight of them, and he doesn't ignore the squirrels, now waiting safely in the branches overhead. Handfuls of peanuts are quickly scooped up, and the squirrels, as easy in the presence of cats as they are with people, sometimes eat their treats perched on René's shoulder. Lastly, René reaches for the pigeon feed. He bends down, then tosses high. The pigeons take flight, flapping madly, snatching bits out of the air before landing on the concrete to clean up the rest.

People have complained about the pigeons from time to time, and René has even been asked to stop feeding them. He responds the same way he's always responded to complaints about his work with the animals. He ignores them. Although everyone on the Hill knows him, not everyone values what he does for the cats, and he's fully aware of this. From the government, the best he can hope for is that they continue to tolerate the cats' presence. Official support would be too controversial, so not a dime of taxpayers' money goes toward the cat sanctuary in spite of the fact that it's mentioned in the official pamphlet and on a Government of Canada website, A Treasure to Explore, Parliament Hill, Ottawa, Ontario, Canada:

Cat Sanctuary

Tucked away in the trees that border the rear of Parliament Hill is a small community of stray cats. This area, which has now come to be called the "Cat Sanctuary," has been home to strays since the late 1970s. A volunteer ensures that the shelters used by the cats are maintained and that the animals are fed every day.

The contrast between these modest shelters and the formality and tradition of the Parliament Buildings is a symbol of compassion, one of the important elements of Canadian society.

This anonymous "volunteer" doesn't let such nice-sounding but essentially empty sentiment get in the way of the job he's there to do. Nor does he let resentment mar his day. He talks to the animals as he works, scolding, cajoling and laughing, simply living in the moment, oblivious to the bureaucracy that sizzles and bubbles all around him.

Over the course of the afternoon, René fills each individual dish as often as necessary and freshens the water supply. After the first feeding frenzy has subsided, René leans against the shelter and surveys his charges, checking for signs of illness or injury. He knows each of them. The big orange and white male, Brownie, is the boss. If necessary, Brownie doesn't hesitate to put another cat in its place with a well-placed swat. But even Brownie doesn't mess with Big Mama. René says she's the most senior of the bunch, at least 20 years old. She spends her days sleeping—on a chair in the sun or inside a shelter if it's cold or wet. Fluffy, the friendly grey and white tabby, seems to be the public-relations consultant of the group. He goes up to anyone who will pet him, giving a quick rub and purr before going on to glad-hand another member of the crowd. But Blackie hovers around René even after the meal is over. He clearly enjoys the attention from his benefactor and is reluctant to stray far from him.

The cat shelters at Parliament Hill. ROXANNE WILLEMS SNOPEK

The cats look a little on the rustic side—twigs cling to Fluffy's tail, and when one of the calicos rolls over for a tummy rub, she reveals white fur stained yellowish from the straw—but they appear as healthy and happy as most house cats. They are certainly well fed. René makes sure of that.

In addition to dry kibble, he puts down a variety of other edibles, including different flavours of canned food and a few semi-moist treats. René spends an average of $6,000 a year supporting the cats—a substantial amount on his pensioner's fixed income. The cats finish their meals, settle down for a nice after-dinner wash, and gradually melt away into the background once again.

René relies on donations to help with expenses. A lockbox is bolted to the metal fence near his area, with a sign explaining the history of the sanctuary. The offerings rarely amount to much, but he is grateful for whatever assistance he receives. One year he was excited to learn that a major pet-food manufacturer had agreed to donate a substantial amount of food to the sanctuary, with the possibility of becoming a long-term supporter. The long-term part didn't pan out, but René isn't one to look a gift horse in the mouth. Veterinary care, the next big expense after food, is no longer an issue thanks to the generosity of the veterinarians and staff at Alta Vista Animal Hospital. All the cats are spayed or neutered and fully vaccinated. If René suspects one of the cats may be feeling under the weather, he contacts the staff and someone comes to pick up the cat in question.

This support has ensured that the cats' health needs are looked after, relieving René of his biggest concern. But even if no one ever stepped in to give him a hand, René would keep caring for the cats no matter what. "I'll keep doing this maybe until I'm 99! I feel good." He takes a deep breath and gestures with his arm. "I'm outside, in the fresh air. When I'm with the cats I am happy."

René's calling has cost him more than money over the years. His devotion, for which he received the Heroes for Animals Award from the Humane Society of Canada, has remained unswerving even in the face of huge personal loss. "I have always been faithful to my daily obligation to the animals on the Hill," says René, "even when my beloved wife, Rita, died during the winter of 1990." But René would be the first to say that his cats have paid him back everything and then some. Every throaty greeting rich in contentment reminds him of why he comes back every day.

But who will take over the job when René can no longer care for the cats? He has occasional helpers, but so far no one has committed to a regular schedule, let alone considered shouldering the full responsibility.

René doesn't waste time worrying about it. Perhaps he has faith that when the time comes, the right person will feel called to the task, the same way he was so many years ago. He's been working with the cats on the Hill longer than most politicians will ever be in office. He's taken no sick days, no vacation time and he's never been paid. Neither he nor his cats have any official power or status. But René appears satisfied as he goes about his humble duties. In a culture obsessed with influence, reputation and competition, this is no mean achievement. Some things of value, the cats might be saying, can't be measured in money.

CHAPTER

7

The Making of
Mister Got-to-Go

*"There are few things in life more heart-warming than to be
welcomed by a cat."* —TAY HOHOFF

SITUATED ON THE SPARKLING WATER of English Bay, two
blocks from Stanley Park and five minutes from downtown
Vancouver, the Sylvia Hotel is a lovely place to stay—if you're
on vacation. But writer Lois Simmie wasn't staying at the
hotel for a holiday. It was a welcome change of pace from life
in Saskatoon, Saskatchewan, but it was still work, plain and
simple. She and children's novelist Cora Taylor were under
the gun to complete the final edits on Cora's second novel,
and the deadline loomed ever nearer. "The publisher told us,
'We're going to shut you up in this hotel and you can't come
out until you're finished,'" recalls Lois. She knew they had
to stay on task, but as she walked through the doors into the
lobby after lunch one day, she noticed a grey cat sitting with

the clerk behind the front desk. She'd seen him earlier and wondered where he belonged; now it was clear that he was completely at home. He looked about himself as if to say, "Of course I live here! Every hotel needs a cat like me!"

A lifelong cat lover, Lois couldn't walk past him without stopping to say hello. Since the age of seven, when her father brought home a tiny grey kitten named Tom, she's never been without a cat in her life. "I just fell in love with Tom," remembers Lois. They grew up together; in fact, Tom lived until Lois had a daughter of her own. When Lois reached out to pet the friendly cat on the counter, she couldn't help but remember the grey cat who had meant so much to her.

"What's his name?" Lois asked the front-desk clerk.

"Got-to-Go," the clerk responded.

"*That's* his *name*?" she asked. "How long has he been here?"

"Seven years," the woman answered, rolling her eyes.

"I went straight upstairs and wrote the story of *Mister Got-to-Go* that afternoon." She recalls, "I kept hoping Cora wasn't writing the same story!" Fortunately, Cora was busy working on her novel. When Lois read it to her the next morning, she loved it, but they both knew they had to complete their current project, so *Mister Got-to-Go* was put on hold.

"It sat for at least two or three years in my file cabinet," admits Lois. She submitted it to two or three publishers, but each time the response was the same: no one was interested in another children's story about a cat. Lois wasn't too worried; a veteran of the Canadian writing scene, she was already well acquainted with the slow wheels of publishing. With a stack of books to her credit already, she knew it was a matter of persistence. Most books rack up dozens of rejection slips before finally being accepted. Even a successful track record such as hers didn't guarantee an easier time with the next manuscript.

"I've been all over the map with my writing," Lois admits. In addition to her award-winning children's books, poetry and plays, she's published short stories, full-length fiction and non-fiction. It was one of her adult books, the biography of an RCMP officer turned murderer, that taught her not to take negative comments to heart. *The Secret Lives of Sgt. John Wilson* is a story of obsession and retribution in early 20th-century Saskatchewan, and Lois was justifiably pleased with how it had turned out—until she read a particularly nasty review of it in *MacLean's*. The reviewer condescendingly tore it apart, mocked her credentials and finally dismissed it by saying that this book would probably only be read by a handful of people interested in esoteric prairie history. Adding to her chagrin, a very similar book reviewed at the same time received a glowing recommendation from the same critic.

She tried not to be discouraged, but secretly she wondered if she'd lost the ability to judge her own work. Then, on a flight to Vancouver, she read in the *Globe and Mail* that her book had been shortlisted for the Arthur Ellis Award in the true crime category. Named after Canada's last hangman, this coveted prize is given by the Crime Writers of Canada. Lois had heard of it, but it had never occurred to her that her book could be nominated. Then she noticed that also among the shortlisted titles was the book the reviewer had raved about in the earlier review after panning hers. But the best part was when the awards were announced. "Both books were short-listed for the Arthur Ellis," she says, "and mine won. Sweet!"

Finally, in 1995, Red Deer College Press recognized the potential in Lois' story. They commissioned award-winning children's artist Cynthia Nugent to draw the accompanying illustrations, and before she knew it, Lois was proofing the final manuscript. *Mister Got-to-Go: The Cat that Wouldn't Leave* was about to become a reality.

"One dark and rainy night at the edge of a city on the edge of an ocean," the book begins, "a stray cat came walking down the beach. Across from an old hotel covered with vines, the cat stopped. As he looked at that place, he got a strange, warm feeling inside him. 'I think,' thought the cat, 'I am tired of being a stray cat.'"

The manager, called Mr. Foster in the book, feels sorry for the cat and decides to let him come in out of the rain—but just for one night. The next morning, he emphasizes, that cat has got to go! But every time they put him out, he finds a way back inside.

Lois was delighted with how perfectly Cynthia Nugent's pictures suited the text. The illustrations faithfully portray the character and dignity of the Sylvia Hotel, complete with its Virginia creeper–covered brick exterior, but it was Cynthia's ability to reveal the cat's emotions that delighted her most. According to the Sylvia Hotel's real-life manager, Axel De Verrier, Got-to-Go was not a cat that suffered fools gladly. Fawning and mincing might earn a hapless admirer a swat on the hand—unless that hand held a tuna sandwich or perhaps a European wiener! He knew how to work a crowd and wasn't above a bit of play-acting if it looked to be worth his while. This wasn't a soft, fluffy lap-kitty. He was a street cat with a tough edge, and Cynthia captured him perfectly. "The reason these books appeal to kids so well, and to such a wide range of ages," explains Lois, "is that they can tell by looking at every illustration what the cat is thinking."

She immediately phoned Cynthia to tell her how pleased she was with the artwork. "I said, 'Obviously, Cynthia, you are a cat person.'" But the illustrator's reply took Lois by surprise. "She answered, 'Hell, no! I had to rent a cat from the SPCA!'" Perhaps this unsentimental viewpoint is what allowed her to so successfully capture the essence of the grey cat's tenacious personality.

The staff of the Sylvia Hotel were naturally pleased to see a book about their cat, but they had no idea how his story would touch the hearts of readers. The hotel had already earned a reputation for pet-friendly accommodation. Built in 1912 and named after the owner's daughter, it was the tallest building in Vancouver's West End for over 30 years and is an attraction in its own right. In 1975, the well-known landmark was given heritage status, ensuring that visitors will be able to enjoy its hospitality for years to come. Now the story of Got-to-Go added a new aspect to its appeal. "They've had busloads of kids come through the hotel to see the cat," says Lois. "There's a whole gallery of Got-to-Go pictures drawn by kids." When the buses pull up to the front doors, the cooks know it's time to put on the hot chocolate.

Lois and Cynthia decided they weren't finished yet; in 2001, Raincoast Books published the sequel, *Mister Got-to-Go and Arnie*. This time, the book describes how the big grey cat's world is turned upside down by the arrival of Arnie, a small, noisy dog whose character is based on the Yorkshire terrier owned by hotel manager Axel De Verrier. Humour and compassion leap off the pages, along with the spectacular West Coast scenery, as Got-to-Go learns to deal with this pesky nap-interrupter. The cat, of course, triumphs in the end.

Lois emphasizes that, while she's taken creative licence with the facts, all adventures are taken from true-life events. No one knows exactly where Got-to-Go came from originally. But Axel clearly remembers his arrival. "Picture this," he says. "English Bay on a rainy October day, a cat enters the Sylvia Hotel and firmly decides to make that place its new home." Employees fell all over the poor cat, fussing about how wet he was, how hungry he looked. Axel told them to get the cat out of there. The cat looked plaintively at the employees and meowed. From then on, Got-to-Go had the upper hand. "I eventually lost the game," says Axel, "and the cat moved in and made the Sylvia Hotel its residence." But he admits he didn't put up much of a fight; he capitulated in a matter of hours.

It was a fortuitous decision for them both. Almost immediately, Got-to-Go began to tailor the job description of "Hotel Cat" to fit himself, giving people one more reason to visit the Sylvia. Local residents often stopped in to say hello and give him a rub, which he might or might not choose to receive graciously. He preferred to greet visitors from his vantage point on the desk while they registered.

"His schedule was very simple," recalls Axel. "He slept during the day, got food from the maids downstairs, woke up in the evening and waited in the old manned elevator until the bellman brought him up to lobby level." From there, the cat went out to see what trouble he could drum up in the neighbourhood, usually staying out for most of the night. Several times he returned battered and bloodied from his nighttime revelries, after which someone would cart him to the animal hospital to be patched up. He often returned to the hotel in the early morning at the same time the newspaper delivery truck pulled up to the front doors. Reminiscing, Axel says, "Then he had a long, extravagant stretch in the middle of the lobby as he waited for the housekeeper to arrive and take him downstairs." Sometimes during warm afternoons the cat drowsed in one of the lobby's sunny windowsills, enjoying the guests' many admiring comments.

It was a golden time in the history of the Sylvia. "Nowadays, a cat wouldn't be allowed in a public eating area. But you always could tell when Got-to-Go came into the dining room because all the diners' heads would turn down at the same time as he wound his way between the tables," remembers Lois.

Discovering and sharing stories like this one is one of the best parts of Lois' work as a writer. "This has been so much fun," she says.

Cats are a recurring theme for Lois. One of her projects, a book titled *What About George?*, is about feral cat rescue and Linda Jean Gubbe's work with Street Cat Rescue of Saskatoon. And Got-to-Go was far from being the first significant cat in her life. Like many writers, she has reserved some desktop space for a number of feline muses. "My former cats have all been great lovers of lying under the desk lamp, watching me type," she says.

Today Lois has a tortoiseshell cat named Alice and a grey and white kitten called Amelia Ann Higgins. Alice had given birth while at the SPCA, and as her kittens grew and found homes, she became lonely. "When her own litter was all adopted out, she kept reaching through the bars toward these cages with kittens in them," says Lois. "So they started letting her care for orphaned kittens." By the time Lois decided to give Alice a home, the cat had fostered about

20 motherless tykes. She'd also developed a great reputation as a mouser. "No wonder she was bored when she came to my place," Lois adds. "She needs company."

Cats have a way of insinuating themselves into a life, regardless of whether or not they are expected. All we can do is accept them for the gift they are, and be grateful.

Got-to-Go may have started his life as a vagabond, but he ended it in the lap of luxury, surrounded by friends. As he got older, he found it hard to keep up his duties as Hotel Cat. "The last time I saw him," says Lois, "they brought him up from behind the furnace, and he was all dusty and annoyed." He craved peace and quiet and tended to spend more and more of his days sleeping in tucked-away places, but he never lost his spirit.

"Despite the fact that he did not like to be petted," adds Axel, "and despite his departure for cat heaven in 1993, our guests still talk about Mister Got-to-Go!" Got-to-Go, the cat that wouldn't leave, had become far more than an old cat. He was a beloved friend who brought something special to thousands of travellers and readers all over the world.

"It's seven years since that dark and raining night the stray cat came walking down the beach to the Sylvia Hotel," the book ends. "Every so often, Mr. Foster says, 'My word, is that cat still here? He's got to go, you know. As soon as it stops raining, that cat's got to go.'

"Sometimes the sun is shining when he says it."

8

Journey's End

"He makes his home where the living is best."
—LATIN PROVERB

KAREN BARKER STOOD IN THE doorway of her new home and looked around. It was July 25, 2003. She'd moved only a few kilometres from her old neighbourhood in Calgary, Alberta, but the house was a huge change. It was newer, bigger and more private. Her mind was filled with plans. First on her list was a backyard fence so her cat, Theo, could explore in safety.

Karen had tried to convince Theo that this new house was a good move, but he wasn't having it. Everything about him oozed resentment, from his luxurious tail, twitching in annoyance, to the glare in his golden eyes. Even his magnificent caramel and cream fur looked rumpled and put out. "Here I was all excited," says Karen, "and Theo wouldn't even come out from under the dining-room table."

She'd expected it would be traumatic for him. The old neighbourhood where Theo had lived with Karen for the past nine years had been very sheltered and safe. "When Theo went outside there, all the neighbours knew him. In fact," she adds, "they all fed him." He'd always been a very confident cat, unafraid of strange noises or new people. Nothing, from the hum of a treadmill to the roar of an engine, caused him to bat an eye. His size, his coat and his easygoing temperament even made Karen wonder sometimes if he was part Ragdoll, a breed with a reputation for becoming extremely relaxed when being stroked. "A typical position for him was to lie half on the couch and half hanging off of it."

A bit of upset was to be expected, but Karen was confident Theo would get over it as soon as he discovered how nice the new place was. She gently encouraged him to explore the yard, carrying him outside with her. But he wasn't interested. As soon as she set him down, he dashed for shelter beneath the nearest object and refused to come out. "It wasn't like him to be so out of sorts," she says. Karen was beginning to realize Theo was seriously upset by this move.

"Before, you could tell he didn't know what to do with himself, but at least he'd been affectionate," she recalls. "That day he kept glaring at me, as if he was angry." When she reached out to stroke him, he grumbled at her and stalked away. Karen hoped he'd soon come around. Even if Theo didn't realize it, Karen knew he didn't really have a choice.

They weren't moving back. Giving him to a friend from the old neighborhood wasn't an option. Seeing him so miserable made her feel wretched too, but to be apart from him was unthinkable. She didn't know what to do; Theo simply had to adjust. "I don't have any family nearby," explains Karen. "My half-sister lives on the other end of the country, and my parents are dead. This cat is my everything."

But on August 5, his annoyance moved into a whole new realm. It had been a fairly typical day: Karen had gone to her job as a service coordinator, come home and then gone out to do a bit of shopping. "I came home about 10:15 that evening. As soon as I opened the door, Theo dashed out between my feet." She was surprised, but told herself not to worry. He'd been outside a few times with her, so she knew he was at least somewhat familiar with the area. She put down her shopping, hung up her jacket and then went around to the backyard, hoping to find him there and cajole him into returning to the house. But he wasn't there. She went back to the front. No Theo. Where could he have gone in such a short time?

Karen walked all around the house, calling and shaking the cat-food box. Finally she decided to wait inside for him to come back. "I thought I'd leave the back door open and run the can opener a couple of times," she says, "because that usually worked." Still he didn't come home. At about 2 a.m., Karen went to bed, a hard knob of dread forming in her stomach. She might as well have stayed up, because she couldn't sleep for listening. She got up to check the doors every hour and even went out to walk up and down the alley. But there was no sign of him, nothing to indicate he'd even been there. "It was as though aliens had picked him up off the face of the earth. He was just gone," she says.

When Karen got up to go to work the following morning, the full realization of Theo's disappearance hit her. His food dish sat untouched. His favourite spots lay empty. "Nothing worse could have happened to me," she says. Panic began to set in, but she pushed it down and tried to focus on her responsibilities.

Karen coordinates support services for people with disabilities. Her network of friends and colleagues is wide, and it didn't take long for everyone in her office to hear the news that Theo had gone missing. Newcomers only had to look at the pictures on Karen's desk to know Theo was important to her. Karen tried to concentrate on her work, but worry kept intruding.

Locating Theo became the nucleus of her life, and working to bring him home kept her from despair over his possible fate. Her first task was to get the word out. Across the city of Calgary, Karen's posters began to appear, all bearing the same message: MISSING! The posters had a picture of Theo, his tattoo number and Karen's contact information. The same poster hung on her office door where everyone who passed by would be sure to see it.

Then she picked up the phone. Karen contacted the

Calgary Humane Society, as well as every shelter and veterinary hospital she could think of, to give them Theo's identification details. She signed up with CanadaStrays. com and PetLynx.net, two online lost-and-found pet services. Her heartfelt messages drew sympathy from many people, as did her persistence.

Day after day, Karen posted the same plea: "I have lost my beloved cat, Theodore. I check your phone line every day, and have since he went missing. If you see my cat come through your doors, please, please, please call me or email me. Theodore is a nine-year-old ginger and white tabby longhair, with four white feet and a white mane. He is a tad overweight. He has a tattoo in his right ear: CH563. He is the love of my life, my only family."

As the days turned to weeks, Karen established an unvarying morning routine. She'd get up, log on to the websites and scan the photos of any cats that had been found. Then she'd phone the City of Calgary animal services department. Each time she was given the same answer: Sorry, haven't seen him. Finally she'd make the phone call she dreaded most, to the city's road maintenance department. "Sometimes I couldn't actually phone road maintenance, I'd have to get someone else to do it," confesses Karen. If Theo had been killed in an accident, she needed to know. But hearing such news from a harried municipal clerk didn't bear thinking of. Their businesslike attitude toward animals found dead on the road was more than she could take.

· "I dreaded getting those email messages that started out with 'Sorry Karen, but . . .'" says Karen. "My hope constantly waffled. Some days I'd tell myself that Theo was spoiled rotten—a mama's boy who wouldn't be gone long." Then she'd remember Nose Hill Park, the nearby wilderness that's home to a variety of wildlife including deer and coyotes. She tried not to think of the stories she'd heard about coyotes coming into residential neighbourhoods to prey on pets, but as the summer waned and fall approached, she knew it was a very real possibility for Theo.

It had been over a month since he disappeared. "After Theo went missing, I'd go to the humane society every day," says Karen. "First I'd check the room with the lost and found pets, then I'd check the ones for adoption." She came to recognize some of the animals, especially those who stayed longer, but she was too focused on finding Theo to be tempted by any other cat. Then one day while she was making her way through the room, a beautiful little cat named Mini caught her eye. She looked at the cage card and discovered that Mini was 10 years old. The shelter workers told her no one wanted Mini, in spite of her sweet personality, because she was too old. "I thought, 'This is a cat that Theo could get along with . . . if he comes home,'" says Karen. "And I missed having a cat around. So I adopted her."

Mini was a great comfort, but loved ones are irreplaceable. Karen's grief, anxiety and fear for Theo continued to grow. "One night I just absolutely broke down," she recalls.

"I went and sat down by the back door, where I kept checking to see if he'd come home. I sat there till it was dark and just cried and cried."

As she sat weeping in the darkness, Karen realized one thing. If she knew for sure that Theo was dead, she'd be able to mourn. But without that certain knowledge, she couldn't give up, even though the constant bouncing between hope and anguish left her emotionally exhausted. Through her tears, Karen begged every power in the universe for something, anything, to keep her hope alive. "I said, 'I don't know who's running this, God or energy or whatever, but could you just give me a sign that he's okay and that he's going to come home.'"

The next day at work, Karen was surprised to find, addressed to her, a little gift in the inter-office mail from a co-worker she knew only casually. It was a key chain and on it were the words "I Love My Cats." "It wasn't like her to buy me something," says Karen. "But she told me she'd seen it in the store and immediately thought of me, so she bought it." Karen read it again. Cats. Plural. Suddenly her senses went on full alert. It was the sign she'd been looking for, a nudge from the universe telling her to hang in there.

Karen still had many reasons to give up hope. Theo had been gone for more than two months. It was nearing the end of October, and the weather was getting cold. Even if he were alive, he was likely to be ill or injured. But she set those thoughts aside. Instead, in her heart grew the small, insistent belief that she simply had to keep faith and be patient. "I understood then what people say about getting through something a day at a time, or an hour at a time," says Karen. "It was just a matter of getting through it."

Then the calendar turned over. Again. November had arrived, and Theo was still missing. The cold air swirled in from the mountains, adding a welcome crispness to the air and warning of snow soon to come. Some people were already beginning to talk of Christmas. Karen continued her unvarying routine of phone calls and checking websites, and she continued to believe. But with each day and each drop in temperature, it became harder not to grow frantic.

By this time, Theo's disappearance was also registered with the Meow Foundation, the *Calgary Herald*, Shaw Cable and Pets for Life. Karen took out ads in the paper, and while none of the people who read them phoned to say they'd found Theo, she got many calls of support. Some callers were in tears, just wanting her to know they were thinking of her and praying for Theo's safe return. Karen was grateful for every response she got, even the negative ones, because it meant that people were looking. Who knew what chance observation might bring him home again?

Remembrance Day arrived. Karen's parents had been in their early forties when they adopted her. Because they'd both been through the Second World War, Remembrance Day always had special significance in their lives. Even after they'd passed away, Karen honoured the day because she knew how important it had been to them. Throughout the day she said little prayers, hoping that somehow, somewhere, her parents could hear her and send their love to strengthen her. She'd never needed it more.

When she returned home after work that day, the message indicator was flashing on her phone. Karen still has the message. It was from a woman in Okotoks, a small town about 18 kilometres south of Calgary. "My name is Gabby," the voice said in a thick German accent. "I am calling about a cat named Tee-o-dore. Tattoo number CH563. If you are the owner of this cat, please call me. He's very thin, and he's not very happy." As soon as Karen heard the name and tattoo number, she began leaping up and down. As she dialled the number with trembling fingers, the thought uppermost in her mind was, "This is a cat that grew up with a silver spoon in his mouth, and he's been roughing it all this time. No kidding he's not happy!"

Gabby, who ran the Okotoks Pound Rescue, gave directions, and then Karen ran out of the house, forgetting her purse in her haste. All she could think of was getting to Theo as soon as possible. Unfortunately, in her excitement she made a few wrong turns and the trip took about three times longer than it should have. Karen ended up in a nearby town and had to ask for more directions. Finally she pulled up to the right building. Her prayers were about to be answered, but instead of the surge of emotion she expected, she felt calm and peaceful. She didn't know what condition Theo would be in, but at least he'd be back with her. "Gabby met me at the door," remembers Karen. "She took me into a little room, and there was Theo, hiding under a bench." The Theo she'd known in her old house didn't hide; he was more likely to lie on his back with all four feet in the air. She called to him, but it took several tries before he responded. He tentatively peered out, as if unable to believe his eyes, then edged a bit nearer. Softly, Karen started singing to him, something she'd done all his life. She sang, "Who's Afraid of the Big Bad Wolf," and suddenly Theo was purring. "Gabby couldn't believe it," says Karen. "He had been terrified. Then I come in and after a couple of words, he's mama's boy again."

Gabby explained that Theo had shown up at a farm in Okotoks in October. A kindly couple brought him into their garage, fed him and started trying to find out where he came from. Finally they called Gabby, who put her own network into action. Soon after, the trail led to Karen. Karen and Gabby speculated on the many things that could have happened to Theo. Perhaps while Theo was out he had been caught in a cat trap, driven out of the area and dumped on a country road. Or maybe, during his angry spell, he'd made his way inside one of the many RVs or campers in Karen's new neighbourhood and gone for an unexpected ride. They had no way of knowing, and Karen didn't care. All she knew was that her little boy was finally back with her, safe and sound.

His adventure had taken its toll, though. His body had gone from 17 pounds of muscular feline grace to an emaciated

6 pounds. All his bones were clearly visible beneath his skin, and his once-glorious fur was now little more than straggly tufts. He looked fragile, beaten. "Normally," says Karen, "he's a big cat with a lush coat. He looks like he's got bloomers on his legs. When I finally found him, his legs were like sticks and there were no bloomers anymore, just matted bits of fur." Would her old Theo still be there inside this pathetic shell? Karen drove home slowly and carefully with Theo curled up quietly in her lap the whole way, hoping he hadn't been irreparably damaged. "When we got home and I opened up the door, he went in immediately and recognized the place," says Karen. "He went straight to his food dish. He got the bare essentials in—food and water—right away."

"And then he saw Mini." Theo stopped dead in his tracks, assessing the interloper. Perhaps in his time away he'd learned that resisting change is a risky proposition; maybe he was just tired. Either way, he had more important things to do than fight. The cats exchanged unpleasantries then studiously ignored each other.

Over the years, Karen and Theo had developed many rituals. Their usual nighttime routine had always included a cuddle, a wash and a game of "Tent" under the covers; then Theo would settle down for the night. But would Theo remember this much of his old life? Karen watched him, hoping he hadn't forgotten their customary game. "I got ready for bed, and he got into bed with me," says Karen, "and then it was like he hadn't even left. He wanted to play 'Tent.'"

Theo was finally home. Karen's ordeal was over, and her life returned to normal. "Of course, I was so happy. I don't think I've ever been so happy!" Then came the welcome task of informing everyone that Theo was home. She immediately tore down the MISSING! poster on her door and put in its place a banner saying FOUND! The entire office celebrated with her. "Everyone had taken it very personally," she says.

Unbelievably, Theo had no health repercussions from his time on the run. His weight gradually returned to normal, and if anything, he's a little overweight again. Karen says it's as if he's afraid to let himself get hungry and keeps continually trying to make up for the weeks of starvation he lived through.

Theo was gone for 99 days. He returned home on Remembrance Day. It's little details like these that Karen remembers with gratitude. She's kept many of the messages of hope sent to her by friends and strangers, and she's also kept the messages she sent herself. In her darkest moments, when her faith was weakest, affirming the love she shares with Theo was the only thing that helped her through.

> Mummy misses her little boy,
> And Theo needs his mum,
> But he is safe and he is sound,
> And home he soon will come.

Journey's End

Mum will feel his soft warm fur,
And hear his sweet meows,
Theo will lie in mummy's arms,
Again in our new house.

Fate will bring my boy to me,
Love will bring him home.
He'll be fine and he'll be happy
No more will he roam.

9

The Cat Who Stayed for Dessert

"Cats look beyond appearances—beyond species entirely, it seems—to peer into the heart." —BARBARA L. DIAMOND

WHEN I WAS STUDYING TO become a veterinary technician, I worked weekends as an aide at a nursing home. It paid well—better in fact than my first job in a private veterinary practice—but caring for the elderly is not for the faint of heart. The deterioration of aging human bodies is difficult to witness, and even harder to watch is the mental decline. The more skilled aides had a special kind of patience that I believe came from recognizing that, eventually, we all return to infancy. But the very best of them had something more: an understanding that even though dementia has seemingly stripped a person bare, she is still worthy of being treated with dignity. She may still have something to teach.

Today, most nursing homes have a cat or a budgie, or at

least a tank of tropical fish, but back then, the therapeutic value of companion animals for the elderly was just starting to be recognized. I recall one gentleman who kept a couple of cockatiels in his room, and our head nurse brought her Dalmatian to work now and then, but that was about it. Except for a cat named Bella, who belonged to a co-worker I'll call Jennifer.

One evening, near the end of her shift, Jennifer stomped into the staff room, her scrub top spattered with custard. Being a long-term-care aide was paying her way though nursing school, but she hated it; she'd even begun to question whether she was cut out to be a nurse at all.

"Mrs. Tymchuk threw her tray again," I guessed with heartfelt sympathy. I'd dodged my share of dishes too.

"Now I've got to clean her up before bed," Jennifer muttered, swiping ineffectually at the stains. "To think I could be home watching TV with my cat. The worst thing she does is shed."

She spoke often about Bella, her long-haired tabby. The stray had arrived at her door the previous winter, half-frozen and starving. It had taken Jennifer weeks to earn her trust, but it had paid off. She brought her in to work once to show her off. Bella was a calm, confident, affectionate cat, and I was impressed; she even seemed to enjoy meeting some of the residents. But certified pet visitation had yet to become widespread, and it didn't occur to any of us to be more deliberate about it.

"I'll give you a hand with her bath," I promised Jennifer. "And her husband will be here any minute. She's much better with him. Have you met him yet?"

"Leon? No, but I've heard about him. It's the only word I can understand when she gets going."

Jennifer was sceptical that Mr. Tymchuk could penetrate the dementia clouding his wife's world. He was also in his eighties, stooped and grey, but unlike her, his mind was still razor-sharp. He smiled at Jennifer when he noticed her standing in the doorway.

"Is my beauty acting up for you tonight?" he asked, nodding at the stains on her uniform.

Jennifer shrugged, then nodded. "I'm really sorry to interrupt your visit, but she needs a bath before bed now."

He looked excited at the news. "Please, may I help?"

She glanced at me with a look that said, "It's his funeral," but she quickly accepted his offer.

As I'd hoped, the woman was calmer in the presence of her husband. With him standing by, she allowed us to undress her, wheel her to the tub room and strap her into the lift without incident. Once she was safely in the water, Jennifer began rinsing away the bits of food stuck to Mrs. Tymchuk's neck. But despite our attempts at being gentle, the old woman batted at the washcloth. Jennifer's response was to work more quickly.

"May I?" asked Mr. Tymchuk. He held his hand out for the cloth. "I know she can be difficult."

Jennifer stepped back, saying, "Be my guest."

He began talking softly in Russian. After a few moments, Mrs. Tymchuk began to listen, and the fear and confusion on her face disappeared. Very gently, Leon washed each of her hands. Then slowly and carefully, he washed her arms and shoulders, working his way over the wrinkled, sallow skin. After a while, she closed her eyes and relaxed into the warm water.

"My Nadja," the old man murmured. "You are so beautiful."

Mrs. Tymchuk opened her eyes and murmured back, "My Leon. My love." It was the most clarity we'd ever seen her exhibit, and suddenly we caught a glimpse of the well-loved woman who hid deep within the ruin of Alzheimer's disease.

Leon reclined the lift and released his wife's hair into the water. The old woman sighed with pleasure as he stroked and lathered and rinsed. He kissed her temple. "All done, my beauty."

Together, we got her dried and dressed, and Jennifer ordered up a bedtime snack from the kitchen. The woman hadn't eaten her dinner, after all. Then Leon, looking exhausted, sat in the chair next to the bed and motioned for Jennifer to take a seat as well. She glanced at her watch briefly. Her shift was almost over.

"Just for a few minutes," said Leon, reaching for his wife's hand. "I'd like to tell you a story."

"I've heard it," I whispered. "You should stay."

Jennifer sighed, then sat down.

"We've been married for almost 49 years," he began, his gaze lost in the distance of memory. "When we started out, life on the farm was harder than you can imagine. The drought killed our crops, and there wasn't enough grass for the cattle. Our children were small, and I didn't know how we would survive the winter. I felt so helpless, and it made me angry. I was very hard to live with that year. Nadja put up with my moods and left me alone, but one night I came inside to discover she'd taken in a cat."

He chuckled at the expression on Jennifer's face. "That's my Nadja for you."

She looked astounded at the thought she and Mrs. Tymchuk—Nadja—could have something in common.

"The children were so excited," continued Mr. Tymchuk. "They were feeding it custard. You need to understand, Nadja sold most of our eggs and milk. Custard was a special treat, and they were feeding it to a cat. A cat! I was so angry that I picked up a plate and threw it against the wall and stormed out to the barn. I don't know how long I stayed there, but around sundown, Nadja came out to find me. She knew it wasn't about the cat. 'Leon,' she told me, 'you are not alone in your troubles. I promised to stand by you through everything life brought our way. But if you won't let me, then you have got to go.' She had tears in her eyes, but her voice was firm. 'When you are ready to be with us again, we are here.' Then she kissed my cheek and walked back to the house.

"I stayed in the barn that night, and the next day I headed into town to look for a job." Leon's voice had grown shaky and his eyes shone. "There was nothing, of course, but I kept looking. After about a week, I gave up. I felt like a complete failure, as a farmer, as a husband, as a father. As a man. I started for home, not knowing if I'd be welcome, but I didn't have anywhere else to go. When she saw me coming down the lane, Nadja came out running, her apron strings flying. She threw her arms around me and began to weep. I clung to her like a newborn baby. She just stroked my head and held me. Then we went into the house, as if nothing ever happened.

"If she could stay with me during the hardest time of our life, the least I can do is comfort her now. And remind her of the good times we had."

Leon's eyes never left his wife's face. "From that time on, we always had a cat in the house. I think she misses that some days."

Suddenly Jennifer pushed back her chair. "My shift is over," she said, dabbing at the corner of her eye. "But I'll be back in a half-hour. Can you wait? There's someone I'd like you to meet."

Bella came to work with Jennifer regularly after that and spent much of her time curled up at the foot of Mrs. Tymchuk's bed. The old woman evidently took pleasure in the company of her new friend, and she even stopped yelling and throwing things, lest she frighten Bella away. Bella, in turn, thrived under all the attention.

But the cat was not just thriving. A few months later, Jennifer said, "She's getting fat!"

Sure enough, when I stroked her luxurious, fluffy coat, I felt a comfortable layer beneath that hadn't been there before. Jennifer was mystified; Bella was notoriously picky and rarely even took treats. Plus, her new social life provided more exercise and stimulation.

Then one day, as Jennifer and I were collecting meal trays, she beckoned to me quietly. We peeked around the door as the Tymchuks finished their lunch, and it all became clear. Bella politely licked clean the spoon that Mrs. Tymchuk held out to her, then hopped off the bed and walked to where Mr. Tymchuk was holding out his mostly finished bowl.

Bella had developed a taste for custard.

10

The Simon Years

"No, heaven will not ever heaven be, unless my cats are there to welcome me." —UNKNOWN

ONE MORNING, AS I WORKED my way through the wards of the veterinary hospital in Saskatoon, Saskatchewan, changing litter pans and filling food and water dishes, I asked myself for the millionth time if this was what I went to school for. "I'm a veterinary technician. I should be doing treatments, anaesthetics, laboratory analyses. Instead," I muttered to myself, "I'm cleaning kennels."

I came to the area where the smaller dogs were hospitalized. At the back of one cage crouched a tiny kitten, its striped orange fur matted with food. When he saw me, his mouth opened soundlessly and he tottered over to the bars. He was perhaps four weeks old, too young to be vaccinated. That explained why he was in the dog ward instead of with the other cats—to protect him from the organisms carried by his own species. The kitten sneezed violently, falling off his feet with the effort. He had a serious respiratory infection, but his health was the least of his problems. I glanced at the cage card: Stray. "Oh, boy," I murmured to the little face pressing itself against the bars. "It doesn't look good for you."

The kitten stayed on the ward and recovered slowly, but he remained bedraggled. At first sight, little about him was appealing. His coat was sparse, his face a splotch of ginger on white. Mackerel tabby markings etched hollow flanks and climbed a thin crooked tail. His front end was caked with food, his back end with diarrhea. He smelled terrible.

But every morning when I came to clean, feed and medicate him, he met me with an unmistakable welcome. A disproportionately loud purr rattled from his tiny throat as he tripped over himself in eagerness to rub my hand. He was the ugliest kitten I'd ever seen, but he had character.

His health improved eventually, but he still had no home to go to, no owner to take responsibility for him. One day I overheard the clinicians discussing euthanasia. "I'll take him," I blurted, without thinking. I wasn't supposed to have pets in my apartment, but I figured I'd only keep him until I found him an owner. That evening I trekked across campus to the bus stop with a kitten nestled in my backpack, bouncing gently against the towel I'd tucked in with him. Once settled in my seat, I peeked in to find him curled up contentedly, totally unconcerned about the jostling and bumping. He looked up at me calmly, as if to say, "I know I'm in good hands." That night he slept wedged up tightly against my side, his purr reverberating throughout my small apartment.

Within a few days, I knew for certain that no one would ever want this kitten. At the shelter even the cute ones don't always find homes; an ugly, scrawny one like this had no chance. My heart ached for him. Love pours out in abundance to the pretty, the talented, the strong and smart. But what about the ones who stumble on the cracks of inadequacy, overlooked and bypassed until even a mere trickle of affection is too much to expect? Eventually they learn that all life holds for them is rejection. They give up hoping for anything more.

Well, this creature simply refused to give up. He was blissfully unaware of his outlandish appearance and general lack of appeal. When he scrambled awkwardly into my lap at the end of the day, his raucous purr high in his throat, he seemed convinced that he was the best thing to ever happen to me. It didn't take long before I began to believe it too. I knew that there must be some reason he'd fallen into my life. Rules or no rules, I'd found him a home. With me.

If he were to stay with me he'd need a name. That was a poser. Nothing cute or fluffy, obviously. Nothing overly regal or cool. He needed a solid name, not fancy but sturdy, something that would reflect the character I sensed within. One day it just popped into my head: Simon. That was his name. It fit like a glove.

Intensely food-oriented, Simon loved to investigate my meals. One day he stuck his nose into my bowl of hot chicken soup. Sneezing mightily and licking his scalded muzzle in surprise, he retreated, glaring at me as if I should have warned him.

He quickly learned my routine, complaining loudly whenever I gathered my coat and keys to leave. Running from door to window, he would watch me walk away, yowling with forlorn persistence. When I returned at night, his strident call was the first thing to greet me. His warm body winding around my legs was a welcome change from the quiet apartment I was used to, and I discovered I liked my demanding new roommate. He was my buddy, my Simey.

Other changes were happening in my life that winter. I was transferred to the veterinary surgery department and began to really enjoy my work. And a young veterinary student caught my eye: Ray, with his easy laugh and gentle touch with the animals, soon held all my attention. Poor Simey was relegated to the back burner.

It was the start of a long love-hate relationship for Simon and Ray. Slimy, as Ray called him, delighted in ambushing Ray from around corners and behind doors. Grappling with all four paws, he'd pummel poor Ray's ankles then dive back under the couch, waiting for the next attack opportunity. Every encounter ended in a new scratch for Ray. He tolerated the abuse, but he was convinced I had a seriously demented cat. I figured Simon was something of an acid

Simon (bottom), Tabitha (right) and Cody (top). ROXANNE WILLEMS SNOPEK

test; if this guy stuck around in spite of my cat, maybe he was a keeper.

Within months, I had my answer. Simon and Ray became buddies, and I knew Ray and I were meant for each other. As soon as Ray graduated, he and I left the prairies for Ontario. My parents were elected to watch over Simon until we sent for him. Unfortunately, we'd no sooner arrived than I had to go into hospital for a badly needed tonsillectomy. Homesick and in pain, I was lying on the couch when Ray arrived home from the airport with my cat. Doped up on painkillers, I hadn't noticed how late they were. Simon, it turns out, had been misplaced at the airport. His crate had been shunted around from terminal to terminal while Ray frantically chased down the clues, always a few steps behind, hoping he wouldn't have to return empty-handed. Finally they located him, and Ray loaded him into the car. The whole way back, Simon sat plastered against one end of the crate, his eyes wide with fright.

When they walked through the door, Simon took one look at me, dove for my lap and went to sleep. He stayed there the full week I was recuperating, uncharacteristically calm and sedate, seeming to know I needed him. But as soon as I had recovered and was back at work, Simon returned to his wild ways.

Before we knew it, we were married and expecting our first child. One day Ray brought home a most beautiful kitten, a long-haired male we named Cody. He'd been found on the side of the road with a broken leg and brought to the clinic where Ray worked. Ray fixed the leg, knowing that if no one claimed him he'd have to bring him home. Simon loved him. In fact, he loved him so much we had to protect Cody from Simon's exuberant embraces in order to let Cody's leg mend. By the time the little bones had knit and the hair had grown back, he'd grown into a graceful, stunning orange and white prince, the perfect foil for his bumbling adopted brother.

Soon, life changed again with the birth of our daughter

Stephanie. I was worried how Simon would behave around the baby, but he dispelled my fears. He was so happy to have me around during the day, it was worth sharing me with a noisy little human. Although I missed the animals and my co-workers, I loved being home with my child and my Simey.

Time passed. We moved to British Columbia and had another daughter, Andrea. Simon casually reigned over the multitude of pets that collected in our home over time, from cockatiels and baby crows to a retired racing greyhound. Our unusual, unwanted and much-loved cat continued to dip his crooked tail into every teacup, startle every visitor and lick any available chin. He was irritating, always trying to get outside, jumping up and knocking things over. But he'd become part of the fabric of our lives. I couldn't imagine life without him.

Then one day he disappeared.

I was horrified. Simon, my innocent, indoor cat, had escaped unnoticed. His knowledge of the world was limited to the view from the window, and now he was lost. He must be cold and afraid. Perhaps he was injured or even dead.

"Have you seen Simon?" I asked Gertrude, my next-door neighbour.

"It's the weirdest thing," she answered, frowning. "I saw a cat just like him on my way to work yesterday."

In fact, Gertrude had witnessed an altercation between Simon and her own cat in her carport. After a bit of hissing and spitting, Simon had run beneath her car and that was the last time she'd seen him. Several hours later, Gertrude left for work. At a busy intersection, she'd heard the thump of something hitting the pavement underneath her car. When she looked in the rear-view mirror, she saw an ugly orange cat darting through the traffic. "What a coincidence," she thought. "That cat looks just like Simon."

With growing horror, I realized what must have happened. Simon had climbed onto the underside of her car and clung on in fear when it began to move. The area where Gertrude heard the noise was a well-travelled commercial district, with four lanes of busy traffic at all times. If this had been Simon, and if he'd survived, he must be lying somewhere nearby, badly injured.

I was newly pregnant with our third child at that time and feeling less than energetic. But there was no question what we had to do. Stephanie and Andrea and I dashed into the car and headed to the area Gertrude described. We walked up and down the sidewalks, peering under every bush. We rattled his favourite treat can, called his name and asked every person we found.

But no one had seen him. Up one street and down the other we went, all the while dealing with the fears of two little girls who loved an ugly cat that had been with them their whole lives.

Then, success! An ugly orange cat with a skinny, crooked tail? Yup, a woman told us, she'd seen one hiding under the garbage cans behind her house. She'd noticed him because he looked a bit like her own cat—except for his scraggly tail! I moved the cans around and there he was. He greeted me with a plaintive cry, as if to ask, "What took you so long?" He crawled up onto my shoulder, tucked his head under my chin and firmly shut his eyes. If this was freedom, he wanted home.

Stephanie, five, and Andrea, three, were giddy with relief. The bigger miracle, however, was that after riding underneath a car for six blocks, running through four lanes of traffic and spending the night outside in a strange neighbourhood, Simon had not a scratch on him. From that day forward he had no desire to go anywhere near a road. We could let him outside safely now, knowing he'd stay nearby.

As Simon got older, he didn't race to go outside anymore. Instead, he ambled. He no longer jumped from the floor onto my shoulders, and there was a certain stiffness in his hips when he walked that suggested arthritis.

Then, one day, Simon didn't come for breakfast. Alarm bells went off. Simon was not a cat to miss his meals. Ray took him in for tests, and X-rays revealed fluid in his right lung. My husband tried to calm me, but I knew this was a bad sign. He drained some of the fluid and sent it to the lab for analysis while I waited at home, hoping against hope for good news.

The results were unmistakable. Cancer.

Many times I had been on the clinical end of a bad diagnosis, had helped treat sick pets and end the suffering of those beyond hope of recovery. But never before had it been my pet.

I needed to know for sure how sick he was, so we scheduled more tests. An ultrasound revealed that Simon had something wrong in virtually every system of his body. He had heart disease, fluid in his lungs, enlarged kidneys and liver, and bowel and bladder abnormalities. The radiologist said that while Simon's cancer probably originated elsewhere, it had spread to his lungs and possibly to other organs as well. His cardiovascular system couldn't tolerate surgery to find the primary tumour, nor was there any purpose in looking for it. There was nothing to be done. It was just a matter of time now.

It was October when we learned the sad news. "I don't think he'll make it to Christmas," I told our daughters, over the lump in my throat. We decided to hope for my birthday, less than a month away.

So began our last days with Simon. Except for the shaved patch on his chest, he looked relatively normal. He'd never been pretty, so his debilitation wasn't immediately noticeable. But as he got sicker, his appetite dropped more and more until he was barely eating anything. He took to sleeping in warm, tucked-away places, trying in vain to chase the chill of cancer from his bones.

In mid-November, on the morning of my 33rd birthday, Simon climbed onto my husband's chest as we awoke, licked Ray's chin and purred as if all was well. We lay together, stroking his frail body, savouring his loving friendship. It was the last time he ever purred.

Two days later, we awoke to a treat—snow, unusual in our warm province. All day it fell thick and fast, covering the ground as quickly as we could shovel it. The girls were thrilled to have a chance to go sledding and build forts. I picked up Simon to show him the snow, and when I put him down, he could walk only two steps before resting. I picked him up again and carried him to the bedroom, choking back sobs. It was time.

That night after the girls were tucked into bed, I brought Simon downstairs. There, at our kitchen table, Ray brushed back tears and slid a needle into the fragile vein of this ugly cat we'd grown to love. I stroked the ginger fur and kissed the bony head as Simon slipped peacefully from this world. Simon, my Simey, was gone.

It was hard to adjust to his absence. As much as I missed him, it was worse for me to see my daughters grieve. One day, not long after his death, we were talking about Simon. Andrea began to cry and could not stop. We talked about what he had meant to us and how we'd like to remember him. I tried to console her, but my own feelings were still too strong.

Finally, for distraction as much as anything, I suggested we go visit the cats at the local shelter. We dried our eyes and got into the car. As soon as we entered the shelter's cat room, I spotted our reason for coming on that particular day—a four-month-old orange tabby with white markings, a nasty cut on his ear . . . and no time left. If he weren't adopted immediately, he'd be euthanized.

We named him Mylos and brought him home.

Mylos quickly moved into our hearts. Some days I see him sitting in the window, just like Simon did, and the resemblance takes my breath away. He's not a replacement for Simon; he's a reminder that life, and love, go on. Change and loss will always be with me, much as I resist them, but I've learned this truth: when the Simon years come to an end, it means the Mylos years are just beginning.

Epilogue

WE SPRINKLED SIMON'S ASHES BENEATH his favourite cedar hedge, where the birds he loved to watch still nestle in fragrant safety. In January 2004, Simon's old friend Cody joined him at the rainbow bridge. Every spring, the scent of lilac blossoms is rich with memories of our other special old cat.

Our cats have been with us through a lot of living. These days the kingdom of Simon and Cody belongs to Tabitha, Mylos, Sophie and Bryan, and I've no doubt other cats will pass through our home in years to come. But Simon was special. He was the first cat of my adult life, a link between the carefree world of youth and the responsibilities of maturity. The best things in my life all came to me after I opened my home and my heart to an ugly cat that no one else wanted.

Further Information

For further information, see the following websites:

Pacific Animal Therapy Society of Sidney, BC:
　　http://members.shaw.ca/patspets/

Pedigreed cat fancy: http://www.fanciers.com/

Reporting or locating lost animals:
　　http://www.petlynx.net and http://www.strays.ca

SCAT Street Cat Rescue Program Inc, of Saskatoon, SK:
　　http://www.streetcat.ca

Simon Teakettle: http://www.simonteakettle.com

If you would like to help support the cats of Parliament Hill,
　　please contact:

René Chartrand
1207-160 Charlotte St.
Ottawa, Ontario
K1N 8Z5

Acknowledgements

So many feline aficionados contributed to the making of this book! My thanks to Barb Taylor, Linda Jean Gubbe, Barbara Florio Graham, Al and Pat Hodgkinson, Sadey Guy, Caroline Cameron and Nancy Hutchinson, Betty Sleep, René Chartrand, Axel De Verrier, Lois Simmie and Karen Barker for sharing the lives of their cats with me.

An even bigger thank you to my family: Ray, Stephanie, Andrea and Megan. You've fed the cats, made supper, cleaned up the hairballs, vacuumed the floors, walked the dogs and generally supported me royally as my deadline approached. Thank you! (And next time, let's not have any car accidents, dislocated elbows or emergency appendectomies, okay?)

About the Author

Roxanne Willems Snopek has been writing professionally for two decades and is the author of eight books and more than 150 articles. Her non-fiction has appeared in a wide variety of publications, from the *Vancouver Sun* and *Reader's Digest* to newsletters for Duke, Cornell and Tufts universities. In 2006, her novel *Targets of Affection* was published by Cormorant Books. Written under the name RG Willems, it is the first of a new mystery series dealing with the human-animal bond. Short fiction by Roxanne is included in the anthologies *Half in the Sun* (Ronsdale Press, Elsie K. Neufeld, ed.) and *Blood on the Holly* (Baskerville Books, Caro Soles, ed.). Roxanne and her family live in British Columbia, where she is currently at work on her next book.